I0013175

Python Programming for the Global Developer

Leveraging Cross-Platform Tools and Techniques to Create Versatile Software Solutions

THOMPSON CARTER

All rights reserved

Table of Contents

INTRODUCTION

Mastering Python: A Comprehensive Guide for Cross-Platform Development"

Welcome to *Mastering Python: A Comprehensive Guide for Cross-Platform Development*, a book designed to equip you with the knowledge and skills necessary to become a proficient Python developer, with a special emphasis on building cross-platform applications. Whether you are a beginner just starting your journey with Python, an intermediate developer looking to deepen your expertise, or an expert seeking new challenges, this book is tailored to guide you through the diverse world of Python programming, from foundational concepts to advanced cross-platform development strategies.

Python has long been celebrated for its simplicity, readability, and versatility. Over the years, it has grown into one of the most widely used programming languages, powering everything from web applications to machine learning models, and from automation scripts to IoT systems. As software development continues to evolve, the

6

need for applications that seamlessly run across multiple platforms—whether on **Windows**, **macOS**, **Linux**, or mobile devices—has become increasingly important. Python's ability to meet these demands makes it an ideal choice for developing **cross-platform applications**, and this book is dedicated to exploring this exciting field.

In this book, we will dive into the essential concepts and tools you need to harness Python's power for creating applications that work consistently and efficiently across a variety of platforms. Each chapter is carefully structured to build upon the previous one, allowing you to progress from understanding Python basics to mastering advanced techniques for cross-platform development, testing, debugging, and deploying Python applications in real-world scenarios.

What You Will Learn

1. The Foundations of Python: We will start by covering Python's syntax, core concepts, and basic structures. From variables and data types to functions and object-oriented programming (OOP), you will gain a solid foundation that enables you to understand and use Python effectively across multiple projects and domains.

2. Cross-Platform Development: As we move into the core of the book, we will focus on Python's capability to develop cross-platform applications. You will learn how to write code that can run seamlessly across different operating systems and hardware environments. This includes handling platform-specific challenges, using cross-platform frameworks and libraries, and creating applications that can run on **desktops**, **mobile devices**, and even **cloud environments**.

3. Python Libraries and Tools for Cross-Platform Development: Python's extensive library ecosystem is one of its greatest strengths. In this book, we will introduce you to essential libraries and tools that are specifically designed for cross-platform development. Whether it's building graphical user interfaces (GUIs) with **Tkinter** or **PyQt**, developing web applications with **Flask** or **Django**, or leveraging **Docker** for containerized cross-platform deployments, you will discover how to tap into the rich ecosystem Python offers.

4. Testing and Debugging Across Platforms: Ensuring your application runs smoothly across different platforms requires thorough testing. We will explore best practices for testing and debugging Python code in cross-platform

8

environments. You will learn how to use testing frameworks like **unittest**, **pytest**, and **tox**, which can help automate testing across different Python environments, operating systems, and device configurations.

5. Advanced Techniques for Cloud and IoT Development: Python plays a pivotal role in cloud computing, IoT, and serverless architectures. As we move further, we'll look into how Python is used for building and deploying scalable applications in the cloud using platforms like **AWS**, **Azure**, and **Google Cloud**. Additionally, we will dive into the world of **IoT** (Internet of Things) development, where Python's versatility shines as it can be used to program devices, handle sensor data, and communicate across various networks.

6. Ethical and Sustainable Python Development: Finally, we will address the growing importance of ethical and sustainable software engineering practices. We will explore how Python developers can contribute to **green computing**, create **energy-efficient applications**, and develop software that aligns with ethical considerations such as **privacy**, **data security**, and **inclusivity**.

Why This Book?

9

This book is not just about learning Python; it's about learning to build Python applications that can run everywhere—whether it's on your local machine, in the cloud, or on mobile devices. By focusing on **cross-platform development**, we provide you with practical knowledge and techniques that are highly sought after in today's ever-evolving technology landscape. This book is perfect for developers who want to:

- Build applications that can seamlessly run on **multiple platforms**.
- Learn how to manage dependencies and environment setup in a way that works everywhere.
- Understand the challenges and solutions for working with hardware devices and cloud environments.
- Develop scalable, efficient, and sustainable applications.

The world of Python development is dynamic, and the rise of **cloud computing**, **IoT**, and **mobile devices** has created a demand for Python developers who can navigate the intricacies of cross-platform software development. By the end of this book, you will not only have a deeper understanding of Python but also be equipped with the skills to build complex, scalable applications across a wide range of platforms.

Who Should Read This Book?

This book is designed for:

- **Beginners**: If you are just starting with Python, this book will help you build a solid foundation and move quickly to more advanced topics.
- **Intermediate Developers**: If you are already comfortable with Python basics, you will deepen your knowledge in cross-platform development, testing, and deployment strategies.
- **Advanced Developers**: For experienced developers, this book offers new perspectives on Python's role in cloud, IoT, and green computing, and provides advanced insights into creating efficient, scalable applications across platforms.

How This Book is Organized

This book is divided into multiple sections, each focusing on a specific aspect of cross-platform Python development. Each section builds on the previous one, ensuring a smooth progression from fundamental concepts to advanced techniques.

- **Part 1: Getting Started with Python** – Introduction to Python syntax, basic concepts, and tools.

- **Part 2: Cross-Platform Development Fundamentals** – Concepts, challenges, and frameworks for writing cross-platform Python code.

- **Part 3: Libraries and Tools for Cross-Platform Development** – Leveraging Python libraries for GUI, web development, IoT, and cloud computing.

- **Part 4: Testing and Debugging** – How to test and debug Python applications across different platforms.

- **Part 5: Advanced Topics in Cloud and IoT Development** – Building scalable cloud-based applications and working with IoT devices.

- **Part 6: Ethical and Sustainable Python Development** – Addressing the ethical concerns and sustainability in Python development.

- **Part 7: The Future of Python and Cross-Platform Development** – Emerging trends and how Python continues to shape the future of software development.

Final Thoughts

In a world where applications need to work seamlessly across different devices and platforms, Python's flexibility and powerful libraries make it a top choice for **cross-**

platform development. By mastering Python, you will open the door to creating modern, scalable, and efficient applications that can run anywhere. This book is your guide to becoming a proficient Python developer who not only understands the language but can leverage its full potential to build applications that work across **web**, **mobile**, **IoT**, and **cloud environments**.

So, let's begin your journey into the world of Python development and explore the exciting possibilities of cross-platform programming!

Part 1

Introduction to Python and Cross-Platform

Chapter 1

Getting Started with Python

Introduction to Python and Its Popularity in Cross-Platform Development

Python is one of the most popular programming languages in the world, known for its simplicity, versatility, and wide range of applications. It is an ideal choice for both beginner and expert developers due to its clear and readable syntax. Over the years, Python has gained traction as a go-to language for various types of development, including **web development**, **data science**, **automation**, **machine learning**, and, importantly, **cross-platform development**.

Cross-platform development refers to the ability to write software that works across different operating systems (OS), such as **Windows, macOS**, and **Linux**, without requiring significant changes to the code. Python's philosophy of "write once, run anywhere" makes it a perfect candidate for such development. Python code can often be executed on any of these platforms with minimal adjustments, especially with the help of libraries and frameworks designed for cross-platform compatibility.

With Python, developers can build applications that can run on multiple platforms, ensuring a wide audience and maximizing the utility of their software. From desktop applications to web services and even mobile apps, Python's capabilities in cross-platform development are expanding rapidly.

Installing Python on Various Platforms (Windows, macOS, Linux)

To get started with Python, you first need to install it on your system. Python is compatible with all major operating systems, and the installation process is straightforward.

1. Installing Python on Windows:

- Visit the official Python website (https://www.python.org) and download the latest version of Python for Windows.
- Run the installer and ensure that the option to **Add Python to PATH** is checked during installation. This makes Python available from the command line.
- After installation, open the **Command Prompt** and type `python --version` to confirm that Python is installed correctly.

2. Installing Python on macOS:

- macOS usually comes with Python pre-installed. However, you might want to install the latest version.
- Visit the Python website or use **Homebrew** (a package manager for macOS) to install Python. The command for installing Python with Homebrew is:

```
nginx
```

```
brew install python
```

- Once installed, confirm the installation by typing `python3 --version` in the terminal.

3. Installing Python on Linux:

- Most Linux distributions come with Python pre-installed. However, if you need to install or upgrade it, you can do so via the package manager. For example, on Ubuntu, you would use:

```
sql
```

```
sudo apt update
sudo apt install python3
```

- After installation, verify it by typing `python3 --version` in the terminal.

17

After installation, you can begin coding in Python by opening a terminal or command prompt and typing `python` or `python3` (depending on your installation) to start the interactive Python shell.

Python IDEs and Tools for Global Developers (PyCharm, VS Code, etc.)

Choosing the right development environment can make a significant difference in your productivity. Python developers have a variety of **Integrated Development Environments (IDEs)** and **text editors** available to help them write, test, and debug Python code. Some of the most popular tools for Python development include:

1. PyCharm:

- PyCharm is one of the most popular and powerful IDEs for Python. It comes in two versions: the **Community Edition** (free) and the **Professional Edition** (paid). PyCharm offers excellent support for Python development with features like **code completion**, **debugging tools**, and **built-in version control**.
- It also provides **cross-platform support**, so you can use it on Windows, macOS, or Linux.

2. Visual Studio Code (VS Code):

- VS Code is a lightweight, open-source code editor developed by Microsoft. It is highly customizable and has an extensive set of extensions, including those for Python. The **Python extension** for VS Code provides features like **code linting**, **debugging**, and **intelli-sense**.
- One of the key advantages of VS Code is its performance. It's faster and more resource-efficient than some heavier IDEs, making it a good choice for developers who want a more minimalistic environment.

3. Jupyter Notebooks:

- Jupyter Notebooks is especially popular for data science and machine learning tasks. It allows you to run Python code in interactive cells, making it easy to test code, display results, and visualize data.
- Jupyter is also cross-platform, and it runs in a browser, so it's ideal for projects that involve large amounts of data or that require dynamic interaction with code and output.

4. Sublime Text and Atom:

- These are lightweight, open-source text editors with many Python-specific features when paired with plugins. They provide a flexible environment for developers who want a less resource-intensive editor compared to full-fledged IDEs like PyCharm.

All of these tools support **cross-platform development**, allowing you to use the same development environment regardless of whether you're working on a Windows, macOS, or Linux machine.

Running Your First Python Program

Once you have Python installed and your IDE or text editor set up, it's time to write and run your first Python program.

1. Writing Your First Python Program:

- Open your chosen IDE or text editor and create a new Python file (e.g., `hello_world.py`).
- Type the following code:

```python

print("Hello, World!")
```

- This simple program uses Python's built-in `print()` function to display the text "Hello, World!" on the screen.

2. Running Your Program:

- In PyCharm or VS Code, you can simply click the **Run** button to execute your code.
- Alternatively, you can run the program from the command line or terminal. Navigate to the folder where your Python file is saved and type:

```nginx
python hello_world.py
```

or

```nginx
python3 hello_world.py
```

depending on your installation. The output should be:

```
Hello, World!
```

3. Understanding the Code:

- The `print()` function is a built-in function in Python that displays output to the screen.
- `"Hello, World!"` is a string, a sequence of characters enclosed in quotes. When the program runs, Python processes the `print()` statement and outputs the string to the screen.

Congratulations! You've successfully written and run your first Python program. You've also learned about the basic setup for Python development, including installation on various platforms and the tools that are available for cross-platform development. Now that you've taken the first step, you're ready to dive deeper into Python programming and start building more complex, cross-platform applications.

In the following chapters, we will explore more advanced Python concepts, techniques, and tools that will help you leverage Python's power to create software solutions that work seamlessly across different platforms. Whether you're building web applications, desktop software, or mobile apps, Python will be your reliable partner in creating versatile, high-performance solutions.

Chapter 2

The Python Ecosystem

Understanding Python's Core Libraries and the Python Package Index (PyPI)

One of Python's most powerful features is its rich ecosystem of libraries and packages that extend its capabilities. These libraries allow developers to accomplish tasks without having to write code from scratch, making Python an efficient and versatile language for a wide range of applications.

1. Python's Core Libraries:

- **Standard Library**: Python comes with a comprehensive standard library, which means you can perform many tasks out-of-the-box without needing external dependencies. These built-in modules cover areas such as file handling, regular expressions, networking, operating system interfaces, and even working with databases.

  o   Examples include:

- `os`: For interacting with the operating system, such as file manipulation and environment variables.
- `sys`: To access and manipulate system-specific parameters and functions.
- `datetime`: For working with dates and times.
- `json`: For working with JSON data, making it easier to parse and generate data in the widely-used JSON format.

- **Third-Party Libraries**: While Python's standard library is powerful, third-party libraries further extend its capabilities, making Python suitable for a wide variety of tasks. These libraries can be easily installed from the **Python Package Index (PyPI)**.

2. Python Package Index (PyPI):

- **PyPI** is a repository of open-source Python packages that anyone can contribute to or download from. It's the primary source for Python packages, and it houses hundreds of thousands of libraries for practically every use case.
- To install packages from PyPI, developers use **pip**, Python's package installer. For example, to install the

`requests` library (for making HTTP requests), you would run:

```
nginx
```

```
pip install requests
```

- With PyPI, developers can find solutions for everything from web development and data analysis to machine learning and automation. PyPI makes it easy to enhance your Python project by adding the functionality you need with just a few lines of code.

How Python Supports Multi-Platform Development

Python is inherently designed to be cross-platform, meaning that Python code can run on any major operating system without modification. Python programs can be executed on **Windows**, **macOS**, **Linux**, and even **mobile platforms** (with the help of additional tools).

1. Cross-Platform Consistency:

- Python abstracts many of the underlying platform-specific details so that the same Python code can be executed on different operating systems. This makes it

26

easier for developers to create software that works consistently across different environments.

- For instance, the os module provides a consistent way to interact with the operating system, whether you're on a Windows PC, a macOS laptop, or a Linux server.

- Example:

```python
```

```python
import os
print(os.name)
```

This will print the name of the operating system dependent on the platform, whether it's 'nt' for Windows or 'posix' for Unix-based systems (including macOS and Linux).

2. Python for Web and Mobile Development:

- Many Python-based frameworks and tools support building cross-platform applications, such as **Flask** and **Django** for web development, or **Kivy** and **BeeWare** for mobile applications.

- **Flask** and **Django** provide tools to develop robust web applications that can run on any operating system, and can be deployed to cloud environments like **AWS**,

27

Google Cloud, or **Heroku**, where cross-platform compatibility is a must

- **Kivy** and **BeeWare** extend Python to create native mobile applications that run across **Android** and **iOS**, ensuring that Python developers can use their skills to develop applications that work on all major mobile platforms.

3. Python and Virtual Environments:

- Python's **virtual environments** make it easier to create isolated environments for different projects, ensuring compatibility across platforms. This isolation prevents conflicts between different versions of Python packages used in various projects.
- By using tools like **virtualenv** or **conda**, developers can set up an environment for their Python project with specific dependencies and packages, regardless of the operating system.
    - o Example:

```bash

python -m venv myenv
source  myenv/bin/activate    # On
macOS/Linux
myenv\Scripts\activate  # On Windows
```

An Overview of Python's Versatility in Web Development, Data Science, Automation, and More

Python's adaptability makes it suitable for a wide range of applications. It is one of the most versatile languages available, used by developers to create everything from web applications to scientific models, automation scripts, and even video games. Let's explore a few of these major areas.

1. Web Development:

- **Frameworks**: Python has two major web frameworks, **Flask** and **Django**, that help developers build web applications quickly and efficiently.
  - o **Flask** is a lightweight, micro-framework perfect for building small to medium-sized web apps or REST APIs.
  - o **Django** is a full-fledged web framework, offering a comprehensive solution for building large-scale web applications with features like an admin interface, authentication, and a robust ORM (Object-Relational Mapping) system.
- **Cross-Platform Web Hosting**: Python web apps can be hosted on various platforms, from personal servers to cloud platforms such as **AWS**, **Heroku**, and **Google Cloud**.

- Example: A simple **Flask** app to display "Hello, World!" can run on any platform with Python and an appropriate web server (e.g., Nginx or Apache).

2. Data Science and Machine Learning:

- Python is **the language** for **data science**, widely used for processing, analyzing, and visualizing data. Python's libraries like **Pandas**, **NumPy**, **Matplotlib**, **SciPy**, and **TensorFlow** make it a top choice for data analysis, statistics, and machine learning.
- Python can be used for handling and processing large datasets, performing **statistical analyses**, creating **machine learning models**, and visualizing results.
- Example: You can write Python code to analyze a dataset, clean it, build a machine learning model, and visualize the output—all with tools like **Pandas** and **Scikit-learn**.

3. Automation:

- Python is commonly used for **scripting** and **automation** tasks, which can save time and reduce manual effort. With libraries like **Selenium**, **PyAutoGUI**, and **Requests**, Python can automate repetitive tasks such as:
  - Interacting with websites (web scraping).
  - Automating file management.

30

- ○ Sending automated emails or generating reports.
- Example: A Python script using **Selenium** can automate the process of logging into a website and scraping data.

4. Game Development:

- Python is also used in game development, with **Pygame** being one of the most popular libraries. It allows developers to create 2D games and interactive graphical applications.
- Python's simplicity and readability make it an excellent choice for beginners learning game development concepts.
- Example: Creating a basic game where a character moves around the screen in response to keyboard inputs can be done easily with **Pygame**.

5. Internet of Things (IoT):

- Python is a key player in the **IoT** ecosystem, with libraries such as **MicroPython** and **CircuitPython** that enable developers to build IoT applications with microcontrollers (like the **Raspberry Pi** or **Arduino**).

- Example: Python can be used to collect data from temperature sensors, process that data, and send it to the cloud for analysis.

6. Cybersecurity:

- Python is used in cybersecurity for tasks such as **penetration testing**, **network security**, and **malware analysis**. Libraries like **Scapy** and **Requests** are used for network traffic analysis and ethical hacking.
- Example: Writing scripts to scan a network for vulnerabilities or perform security audits.

In this chapter, we've explored the core elements of Python's ecosystem, including the **standard libraries**, the **Python Package Index (PyPI)**, and how Python supports multi-platform development. We also discussed Python's versatility in different fields such as **web development**, **data science**, **automation**, and **game development**. With Python's growing role in various domains, developers are empowered to create software solutions that run on multiple platforms, integrate with different technologies, and serve a wide range of use cases. Whether you're a web developer, data scientist, or automation enthusiast, Python is the language that will help you bring your ideas to life across different platforms.

Chapter 3

Cross-Platform Development: What, Why, and How

Definition and Importance of Cross-Platform Development

Cross-platform development refers to the practice of building software applications that can run on multiple operating systems (OS) or platforms, such as **Windows, macOS, Linux**, and **mobile platforms** like **Android** and **iOS**, without requiring significant changes to the codebase. In simpler terms, cross-platform development allows developers to write code once and deploy it across multiple platforms.

Cross-platform development is essential in today's tech landscape for a few key reasons:

1. **Wider Reach**:
    o By targeting multiple platforms, businesses can reach a larger audience. Software that works across platforms ensures that users, regardless

of whether they are on **Windows**, **macOS**, **Linux**, or **mobile**, have access to the application.

- o For example, a software solution developed with Python for desktop users can reach users on both **Windows** and **macOS**, expanding the user base without duplicating effort.

2. Cost and Time Efficiency:

- o Developing a single codebase for multiple platforms saves both time and resources compared to writing separate applications for each platform. Maintaining one version of the code is also easier than managing several platform-specific versions.

- o For instance, a cross-platform web application using Python and frameworks like **Flask** or **Django** allows developers to target web users across different operating systems.

3. Consistency:

- o Cross-platform development ensures that the application behaves consistently across platforms. This consistency improves the user experience by making the application predictable and easier to use on various devices or systems.

o For example, using Python to develop a cross-platform application can provide the same functionality whether the user is on **macOS** or **Linux**, reducing the likelihood of bugs and compatibility issues.

Challenges and Benefits of Creating Software That Works Across Multiple Platforms

While cross-platform development has significant advantages, it also comes with its own set of challenges. Understanding these challenges and the corresponding benefits is crucial for developing effective cross-platform software.

Challenges:

1. **Platform-Specific Differences**:

   o Every operating system has its unique features, system libraries, file structures, and user interface (UI) conventions. For example, the way a file is accessed or how the user interacts with the app can vary significantly across platforms. Developers must handle these differences to ensure that the application works seamlessly across all platforms.

- Example: File path syntax differs between **Windows** (`C:\Users\Name\Documents`) and **Linux/macOS** (`/home/user/Documents`), which could create issues when accessing files.

2. **Performance Optimization**:
   - Cross-platform applications might not be optimized for each specific platform. While they can function across multiple platforms, performance might suffer if the application isn't fine-tuned for each system. Handling differences in hardware, processing power, and memory between platforms can be tricky.
   - **Example**: An application that runs perfectly on a **macOS** laptop may perform poorly on a **Linux** machine with lower resources, especially if performance optimization has not been taken into account.

3. **User Interface (UI) Design**:
   - Each platform has its own set of design guidelines and UI elements. While some cross-platform frameworks help address these differences, ensuring a consistent and native look and feel across platforms can still be challenging.

o **Example**: A mobile application for **iOS** may have a different navigation style than the same app on **Android**, and ensuring the UI translates well between platforms can take extra effort.

4. **Access to Native Features**:

o Some platforms offer unique features or services (e.g., **macOS**'s **AppleScript** or **Windows**'s **COM objects**) that may not be easily accessible via cross-platform tools. While cross-platform frameworks often include workarounds, accessing the full functionality of each platform's native features might require platform-specific coding.

o **Example**: A cross-platform app that needs to interface with system-level functionalities, like accessing the system tray in **Windows** or managing notifications on **macOS**, may face difficulties if relying solely on a cross-platform framework.

Benefits:

1. **Single Codebase**:

o With cross-platform development, developers can manage one codebase, which reduces redundancy and simplifies maintenance. Fixes, updates, and new features only need to be implemented once, rather than across multiple versions for different platforms.

- o **Example**: A web application developed using Python can be updated on the server side, and those updates will automatically be reflected for all users, regardless of whether they're using **Windows, macOS**, or **Linux**.

2. **Wider Audience and Market Reach**:

- o The ability to deploy an application on multiple platforms ensures that a business can tap into a larger user base. It's especially important for companies that want to target users on both desktop and mobile platforms.

- o **Example**: Developing a Python-powered app for both **desktop** and **mobile** allows a single product to reach users on both **Windows** and **Android**, maximizing the reach without doubling the development effort.

3. **Faster Development and Cost Savings**:

- o By leveraging cross-platform development tools and frameworks, businesses can save time and money by avoiding the need to develop separate versions for each platform. This also leads to faster delivery of updates and new features.

- o **Example**: Using Python and **Flask** to develop a web application that works across both **Windows** and **macOS** allows a business to release new features simultaneously for all users, without additional work for each OS.

4. **Consistency Across Platforms**:

- o Cross-platform tools help create a consistent experience for users regardless of their operating system. Consistency in behavior, features, and appearance enhances the overall user experience.

- o **Example**: A cross-platform Python app using **Tkinter** for GUI development would look and feel the same whether it's running on **Windows** or **macOS**, providing a unified experience for users on different platforms.

Tools and Libraries to Make Your Python Applications Cross-Platform

Python offers several tools and libraries that can help developers build cross-platform applications, enabling them to deploy software on multiple platforms with minimal changes to the code.

1. PyInstaller:

- **PyInstaller** is a popular tool for packaging Python applications into standalone executables. It allows you to create cross-platform executables that work on **Windows**, **macOS**, and **Linux** without needing Python installed on the target machine.
- **How It Works**: PyInstaller bundles your Python application and all its dependencies into a single executable file that can run independently of the platform's Python installation.
- **Example**: Converting a Python script into a standalone Windows executable with PyInstaller can be done with a simple command:

```nginx
pyinstaller myscript.py
```

2. Kivy:

- **Kivy** is a powerful library for building cross-platform **GUI applications**. It allows developers to build applications that work on **Windows, macOS, Linux**, and even **Android and iOS**.

- **How It Works**: Kivy provides tools and widgets for building interactive applications, and it handles the underlying OS-specific details for you.

- **Example**: A simple Kivy application with a button that responds to user clicks:

```python
from kivy.app import App
from kivy.uix.button import Button

class MyApp(App):
    def build(self):
        return          Button(text='Hello,
World!')

if __name__ == '__main__':
    MyApp().run()
```

3. Flask and Django (For Web Development):

- Both **Flask** and **Django** are popular Python web frameworks that allow you to develop cross-platform web applications. Web applications created with these frameworks are platform-independent, as long as you deploy them on a server with Python installed.

42

- **How They Work**: These frameworks allow you to create dynamic websites and APIs that run on various operating systems, with deployment options available for Windows, Linux, and cloud platforms like **Heroku**, **AWS**, and **Google Cloud**.

- **Example**: A simple Flask-based web app that works across platforms by running on a server and being accessible through a web browser.

4. BeeWare:

- **BeeWare** is another framework that allows Python developers to write native applications for **macOS**, **Windows**, **Linux**, **iOS**, and **Android**.

- **How It Works**: BeeWare lets you write Python code that interacts with native platform-specific APIs, enabling you to create cross-platform applications with native look and feel.

- **Example**: Using BeeWare, you can create a desktop app that runs on both **Windows** and **macOS** by writing Python code that communicates with native system APIs.

5. Docker (For Containerization):

- **Docker** is a platform used to develop, ship, and run applications inside containers. It allows Python applications to be deployed consistently across multiple environments, whether it's **Windows, Linux, or macOS**.

- **How It Works**: By containerizing a Python application, Docker ensures that it runs the same way regardless of the operating system, as long as Docker is installed on the target machine.
- **Example**: Running a Python web app in a Docker container ensures that the app works consistently on different platforms without the need for setting up the environment separately for each OS.

Cross-platform development is an essential skill for global developers looking to create software that can reach a broad audience. Python's flexibility, combined with a variety of tools and libraries, enables developers to write applications that work seamlessly across multiple platforms. While there are challenges associated with platform-specific differences, Python's cross-platform tools such as PyInstaller, Kivy, Flask, and Docker help developers create efficient, maintainable, and versatile applications that can run on any operating system. By leveraging these tools, developers can focus on creating high-quality software while ensuring a smooth user experience across various platforms.

Chapter 4

Python Syntax and Fundamentals

Variables, Data Types, Operators, and Control Structures

Understanding the core syntax and structure of Python is essential for any developer. In this section, we'll break down the basic building blocks of Python programming, which include variables, data types, operators, and control structures.

1. Variables:

- A variable is a named location used to store data in the program. Python is dynamically typed, meaning you don't need to explicitly declare the type of a variable.
- You can assign a value to a variable using the assignment operator =. For example:

```python
python

x = 10    # Assigns the value 10 to the variable x
name = "Alice"    # Assigns the string "Alice" to the variable name
```

46

- Python allows you to reassign variables at any time, and the type of the variable will automatically change depending on the new value assigned.

```python

x = 10   # integer
x = "Hello"   # now x is a string
```

2. Data Types:

- **Integers (int)**: Whole numbers, both positive and negative, without a decimal point.

```python

age = 25
```

- **Floating-Point Numbers (float)**: Numbers that contain a decimal point.

```python

price = 19.99
```

- **Strings (str)**: A sequence of characters enclosed in single or double quotes.

```python
```

47

```
greeting = "Hello, World!"
```

- **Booleans (bool)**: Represents True or False values.

```python
is_active = True
```

- **Lists**: Ordered, mutable collections of items.

```python
fruits = ["apple", "banana", "cherry"]
```

- **Tuples**: Ordered, immutable collections of items.

```python
coordinates = (10, 20)
```

3. Operators:

- Python uses a variety of operators to perform operations on variables and values. These include:
  - **Arithmetic operators**:

```python
x = 10
```

```
y = 5
result = x + y  # Addition
result = x - y  # Subtraction
result = x * y  # Multiplication
result = x / y  # Division
result = x // y  # Floor division
(returns the integer part)
result = x % y  # Modulo (remainder)
result = x ** y  # Exponentiation
```

o **Comparison operators** (for equality and inequality):

python

```
result = x == y  # Equals
result = x != y  # Not equals
result = x > y  # Greater than
result = x < y  # Less than
```

o **Logical operators** (for combining conditions):

python

```
result = x > 5 and y < 10  # True if
both conditions are true
result = x > 5 or y < 10  # True if
at least one condition is true
result = not (x > 5)  # True if
condition is not true
```

49

4. Control Structures:

- **Conditional Statements** (`if`, `elif`, `else`):
    - These structures allow you to control the flow of the program based on conditions.

python

```python
age = 20
if age >= 18:
    print("You are an adult.")
else:
    print("You are a minor.")
```

- **Loops** (`for`, `while`):
    - **For loop**: Used for iterating over a sequence (like a list, tuple, string, or range).

python

```python
fruits = ["apple", "banana", "cherry"]
for fruit in fruits:
    print(fruit)
```

   - **While loop**: Repeats as long as a condition is true.

python

```
count = 0
while count < 5:
    print(count)
    count += 1
```

Functions, Loops, and Conditional Statements

1. Functions:

- A function is a block of code that performs a specific task and can be reused throughout your program. Functions are defined using the `def` keyword.
- Example:

```
python
```

```
def greet(name):
    print("Hello, " + name + "!")

greet("Alice")  # Calling the function with
an argument
```

- Functions can also return values using the `return` keyword:

```
python
```

```
def add(a, b):
    return a + b
```

51

```
result = add(3, 4)
print(result)  # Output: 7
```

2. Loops:

- **For loop**: Loops through a sequence or range.

python

```
for i in range(5):  # Loops through numbers
0 to 4
    print(i)
```

- **While loop**: Loops while a condition is true.

python

```
counter = 0
while counter < 3:
    print("Counter:", counter)
    counter += 1
```

3. Conditional Statements:

- Use if, elif, and else to execute different blocks of code based on conditions.
- Example:

python

```
x = 10
if x < 5:
    print("x is less than 5")
elif x == 10:
    print("x is 10")
else:
    print("x is greater than 5 but not 10")
```

Real-World Example: Writing a Simple Python App for User Input

In this section, we'll write a simple Python application that asks the user for their name and age, performs a check, and then prints a personalized message based on the input.

Step 1: Taking User Input:

- Use the `input()` function to get input from the user.
- The `input()` function always returns the user's input as a string, so you may need to convert it to the appropriate data type (like `int` for numbers).

Step 2: Implementing Conditional Logic:

- Based on the user's age, we'll display different messages.

```python
def user_info():
    # Taking user input
```

```
name = input("Enter your name: ")
age = int(input("Enter your age: "))   #
Converting the input to an integer

# Conditional logic based on age
if age >= 18:
    print(f"Hello {name}, you are an adult!")
else:
    print(f"Hello {name}, you are a minor!")

# Call the function to run the program
user_info()
```

Explanation:

1. The function `user_info()` is defined to ask for the user's name and age.

2. The `input()` function collects the name, and `int(input())` ensures the age is converted into an integer.

3. The `if` statement checks if the user's age is 18 or greater and prints a corresponding message.

4. The program displays a personalized message based on the input, making it interactive and responsive to user data.

Example Output:

54

```
yaml

Enter your name: Alice
Enter your age: 22
Hello Alice, you are an adult!
```

In this chapter, we've covered some of the core fundamentals of Python: variables, data types, operators, control structures, and how to define functions. We also demonstrated how to use loops and conditionals in Python to control the flow of a program. Finally, we created a real-world Python application where user input is collected, processed, and used to generate dynamic output.

Understanding these core concepts will provide you with a solid foundation as you continue learning Python. These basics will serve as the building blocks for more complex applications and functionalities, enabling you to tackle more advanced topics in later chapters.

Chapter 5

Object-Oriented Programming (OOP) in Python

Introduction to Classes and Objects

Object-Oriented Programming (OOP) is a programming paradigm that organizes software design around **objects** rather than functions and logic. An object is an instance of a **class**, and classes serve as blueprints for creating objects.

1. Classes:

- A **class** is a template for creating objects, defining properties (called **attributes**) and behaviors (called **methods**) that the objects created from the class will have. Think of a class as a blueprint, and objects are the actual instances created from that blueprint.

Example:

python

```
class Car:
```

56

```
    # Constructor to initialize the object's
state
    def __init__(self, make, model, year):
        self.make = make
        self.model = model
        self.year = year

    # Method to display car information
    def display_info(self):
        print(f"{self.year}            {self.make}
{self.model}")
```

In this example:

- The `Car` class has three attributes: `make`, `model`, and `year`.
- The `display_info()` method prints out the car's details.

2. Objects:

- An **object** is an instance of a class. It's created by calling the class as if it were a function. Once an object is created, you can access its attributes and methods using dot notation.

Example:

```python
python
```

```python
my_car = Car("Toyota", "Corolla", 2022)  # Create
an object (an instance of Car)
my_car.display_info()  # Call the display_info
method
```

Output:

```yaml
yaml
```

```
2022 Toyota Corolla
```

Methods, Inheritance, and Polymorphism

Object-Oriented Programming also involves **methods**, **inheritance**, and **polymorphism**, which allow for more powerful and reusable code.

1. Methods:

- A **method** is a function defined inside a class that operates on instances of that class. Methods can access and modify the object's attributes and call other methods within the class.

Example:

```python
python
```

```
class Car:
    def __init__(self, make, model, year):
        self.make = make
        self.model = model
        self.year = year

    def start_engine(self):
        print(f"The    {self.make}    {self.model}
engine is now running!")

my_car = Car("Honda", "Civic", 2021)
my_car.start_engine()   # Calling the start_engine
method
```

Output:

```
arduino
```

The Honda Civic engine is now running!

2. Inheritance:

- **Inheritance** allows one class to inherit the attributes and methods of another class. This promotes code reusability and creates a hierarchical relationship between classes.

Example:

59

python

```python
class ElectricCar(Car):  # Inherit from the Car
class
    def __init__(self, make, model, year,
battery_size):
        super().__init__(make, model, year)  #
Call the parent class's __init__ method
        self.battery_size = battery_size

    def display_battery_info(self):
        print(f"The battery size of this electric
car is {self.battery_size} kWh.")

my_electric_car = ElectricCar("Tesla", "Model
3", 2023, 75)
my_electric_car.display_info()      # Inherited
method from Car
my_electric_car.display_battery_info()  # Method
of ElectricCar
```

Output:

kotlin

```kotlin
2023 Tesla Model 3
The battery size of this electric car is 75 kWh.
```

- The `ElectricCar` class inherits from the `Car` class, meaning it has access to the `display_info()` method, and we can also add new attributes and methods specific to electric cars, such as `battery_size` and `display_battery_info()`.

3. Polymorphism:

- **Polymorphism** allows different classes to define methods with the same name, but each method can perform different tasks based on the object's class. This makes code more flexible and scalable.

Example:

python

```python
class Car:
    def start(self):
        print("Starting the car engine...")

class ElectricCar(Car):
    def start(self):
        print("Starting the electric motor...")

my_car = Car()
my_electric_car = ElectricCar()
```

```
my_car.start()   # Calls Car's start method
my_electric_car.start()   # Calls ElectricCar's
start method
```

Output:

```
nginx

Starting the car engine...
Starting the electric motor...
```

- Both the `Car` and `ElectricCar` classes have a `start()` method, but each class implements it differently. This is an example of **method overriding**, a common use of polymorphism in object-oriented programming.

Real-World Example: Building a Simple Inventory Management System Using OOP

In this real-world example, we'll build a simple inventory management system using object-oriented programming. The system will consist of two classes: one for managing individual products and another for managing the inventory of multiple products.

Step 1: Define the Product Class

- The `Product` class will store information about a product, such as its name, quantity, and price. It will also include a method to display the product's details.

python

```python
class Product:
    def __init__(self, name, quantity, price):
        self.name = name
        self.quantity = quantity
        self.price = price

    def display_product_info(self):
        print(f"Product: {self.name}")
        print(f"Quantity: {self.quantity}")
        print(f"Price: ${self.price:.2f}")

    def update_quantity(self, quantity):
        self.quantity += quantity
        print(f"Updated quantity of {self.name}: {self.quantity}")
```

- The `Product` class has attributes `name`, `quantity`, and `price`, along with a method to display product information (`display_product_info()`) and another to update the quantity of the product (`update_quantity()`).

Step 2: Define the Inventory Class

- The `Inventory` class will hold multiple products, allowing us to add products to the inventory, display all products, and update quantities when stock is added or sold.

python

```python
class Inventory:
    def __init__(self):
        self.products = []    # List to store
Product objects

    def add_product(self, product):
        self.products.append(product)
        print(f"Added    {product.name}       to
inventory.")

    def display_inventory(self):
        print("\nInventory:")
        for product in self.products:
            product.display_product_info()
            print("--------")

    def            update_product_quantity(self,
product_name, quantity):
        for product in self.products:
            if product.name == product_name:
```

```
product.update_quantity(quantity)
                break
        else:
            print(f"Product   {product_name}   not
found.")
```

- The `Inventory` class holds a list of `Product` objects. The `add_product()` method allows us to add products to the inventory, while the `display_inventory()` method displays all products in the inventory. The `update_product_quantity()` method allows updating the stock of a specific product by its name.

Step 3: Using the Classes to Create the Inventory System

```python
python

# Create Product objects
product1 = Product("Laptop", 50, 999.99)
product2 = Product("Smartphone", 100, 599.99)

# Create an Inventory object
inventory = Inventory()

# Add products to the inventory
inventory.add_product(product1)
inventory.add_product(product2)
```

```python
# Display inventory
inventory.display_inventory()

# Update quantity of a product
inventory.update_product_quantity("Laptop", 10)
inventory.update_product_quantity("Smartphone",
-20)

# Display inventory again
inventory.display_inventory()
```

Output:

vbnet

```
Added Laptop to inventory.
Added Smartphone to inventory.

Inventory:
Product: Laptop
Quantity: 50
Price: $999.99
--------
Product: Smartphone
Quantity: 100
Price: $599.99
--------

Updated quantity of Laptop: 60
Updated quantity of Smartphone: 80
```

```
Inventory:
Product: Laptop
Quantity: 60
Price: $999.99
--------
Product: Smartphone
Quantity: 80
Price: $599.99
--------
```

Explanation:

- We first created two `Product` objects: a laptop and a smartphone, with specified quantities and prices.
- Then, we created an `Inventory` object and added the products to it.
- After that, we displayed the inventory, updated the quantity of the laptop and smartphone, and displayed the inventory again to reflect the updated quantities.

This example demonstrates how to use **OOP principles** like **encapsulation**, **methods**, and **object interactions** to build a simple, real-world application. The `Product` and `Inventory` classes encapsulate the data and behaviors of the products and inventory system, while the inventory system can be easily expanded by adding more methods for managing products.

In this chapter, we've learned the key concepts of **Object-Oriented Programming (OOP)** in Python, including how to define classes, create objects, and work with methods, inheritance, and polymorphism. We also applied these concepts in a real-world example to build a simple inventory management system. By mastering OOP, you can build more modular, maintainable, and scalable software solutions, as well as better understand Python's powerful object-oriented features.

Chapter 6

Handling Data Structures Efficiently

Lists, Tuples, Dictionaries, and Sets

Python offers several built-in data structures that allow developers to store, organize, and manipulate data efficiently. These data structures each have their unique features and are suited for different types of tasks. In this chapter, we will explore four key data structures in Python: **lists**, **tuples**, **dictionaries**, and **sets**.

1. Lists:

- **Definition**: A **list** is an ordered collection of items, which can be of any data type. Lists are mutable, meaning you can change, add, or remove elements after the list is created.
- **Features**:
  - Lists allow duplicates.
  - You can access elements by their index.
  - Lists are dynamic, meaning you can change their size.

69

- o Lists support a variety of methods like `append()`, `insert()`, `pop()`, `remove()`, and `sort()`.

Example:

```python
python

fruits = ["apple", "banana", "cherry"]
fruits.append("orange")   # Adding an item
fruits.remove("banana")   # Removing an item
print(fruits)   # Output:  ['apple', 'cherry', 'orange']
```

2. Tuples:

- **Definition**: A **tuple** is similar to a list but is immutable, meaning once a tuple is created, you cannot modify its contents (add, remove, or change items).
- **Features**:
    - o Tuples are ordered and allow duplicates.
    - o Tuples are faster than lists because of their immutability, making them more suitable for use in scenarios where you don't need to modify the data.
    - o Since tuples are immutable, they can be used as keys in dictionaries, unlike lists.

70

Example:

```python
python

coordinates = (10, 20, 30)
print(coordinates[0])   # Output: 10
# coordinates[0] = 15   # This will raise an error
because tuples are immutable
```

3. Dictionaries:

- **Definition**: A **dictionary** is an unordered collection of key-value pairs. Each key is unique, and values can be accessed using their associated key. Dictionaries are mutable, meaning you can change their contents by adding, modifying, or removing key-value pairs.
- **Features**:
  - ○ Keys must be immutable (e.g., strings, numbers, tuples), and each key must be unique.
  - ○ Values can be of any data type, including lists, tuples, and other dictionaries.
  - ○ Dictionaries are very efficient for looking up values by key, making them ideal for situations where fast access to data is needed.

Example:

71

```python
python

person = {"name": "Alice", "age": 25, "city":
"New York"}
print(person["name"])   # Output: Alice
person["age"] = 26   # Modifying a value
person["email"] = "alice@example.com"   # Adding
a new key-value pair
print(person)   # Output: {'name': 'Alice', 'age':
26,    'city':    'New    York',    'email':
'alice@example.com'}
```

4. Sets:

- **Definition**: A **set** is an unordered collection of unique items. Sets do not allow duplicates, and they support mathematical operations like union, intersection, and difference.

- **Features**:

  o Sets are unordered, meaning the items do not have a specific index.

  o Sets automatically remove duplicates, making them useful when you want to store only unique elements.

  o Sets are mutable, but you cannot change an individual item once it's in the set.

Example:

```python
python

numbers = {1, 2, 3, 4, 5}
numbers.add(6)    # Adding an element
numbers.remove(2)    # Removing an element
print(numbers)    # Output: {1, 3, 4, 5, 6}
```

How to Choose the Right Data Structure for the Job

Each of the data structures we've discussed has its strengths and is suited for different tasks. Knowing how to choose the right one is essential for writing efficient Python code.

1. Use a List When:

- You need an ordered collection of items.
- You need to access elements by their index.
- You expect the collection to change in size (adding or removing items).
- You allow duplicates.

Example: Storing a list of user names where the order matters, or keeping track of a series of steps in a process.

2. Use a Tuple When:

- You need an ordered collection of items that won't change.
- You want to ensure the integrity of the data (i.e., no accidental modifications).
- You need to store the collection in a hashable type (e.g., use as dictionary keys).

Example: Coordinates or configuration data that should not be modified once set.

3. Use a Dictionary When:

- You need a collection of key-value pairs.
- You need fast lookups based on keys.
- You don't mind the collection being unordered.
- Keys must be unique.

Example: Storing user information where you need to quickly access data by a unique identifier like `user_id` or `email`.

4. Use a Set When:

- You need an unordered collection of unique items.
- You need to perform operations like intersection, union, or difference.

74

- You want to eliminate duplicates automatically.

Example: Storing a collection of tags or categories where duplicates are not allowed.

Real-World Example: Managing a Contact Book with Python Dictionaries

Now, let's apply what we've learned by building a simple **contact book** application using Python dictionaries. Each contact will be stored as a dictionary entry, where the contact's name is the key, and the value is another dictionary containing the contact's phone number and email address.

Step 1: Define the Contact Book Class

We'll start by defining a class to manage our contact book. This class will include methods to add new contacts, remove existing contacts, search for a contact, and display all contacts.

python

```python
class ContactBook:
    def __init__(self):
        self.contacts = {}   # A dictionary to
store contacts
```

75

```python
    def add_contact(self, name, phone, email):
        """Adds a new contact to the contact
book."""
        self.contacts[name] = {"phone": phone,
"email": email}
        print(f"Contact       {name}       added
successfully.")


    def remove_contact(self, name):
        """Removes a contact from the contact
book."""
        if name in self.contacts:
            del self.contacts[name]
            print(f"Contact       {name}       removed
successfully.")
        else:
            print(f"Contact {name} not found.")


    def search_contact(self, name):
        """Searches for a contact by name and
displays their details."""
        if name in self.contacts:
            contact = self.contacts[name]
            print(f"Name:       {name},       Phone:
{contact['phone']}, Email: {contact['email']}")
        else:
            print(f"Contact {name} not found.")
```

```python
    def display_contacts(self):
        """Displays all the contacts in the
contact book."""
        if not self.contacts:
            print("No contacts found.")
        else:
            print("\nContacts in your book:")
            for name, details in
self.contacts.items():
                print(f"Name: {name}, Phone:
{details['phone']}, Email: {details['email']}")
```

Step 2: Using the Contact Book

Now that we have our class, we can use it to manage contacts by creating an instance of the `ContactBook` class and interacting with it.

python

```python
# Create a new contact book
contact_book = ContactBook()

# Add some contacts
contact_book.add_contact("Alice", "123-456-7890", "alice@example.com")
contact_book.add_contact("Bob", "987-654-3210", "bob@example.com")
```

```
# Display all contacts
contact_book.display_contacts()


# Search for a specific contact
contact_book.search_contact("Alice")


# Remove a contact
contact_book.remove_contact("Bob")


# Display contacts again to verify removal
contact_book.display_contacts()
```

Output:

```yaml
yaml


Contact Alice added successfully.
Contact Bob added successfully.


Contacts in your book:
Name:  Alice,  Phone:  123-456-7890,  Email:
alice@example.com
Name:  Bob,  Phone:  987-654-3210,  Email:
bob@example.com


Name:  Alice,  Phone:  123-456-7890,  Email:
alice@example.com


Contact Bob removed successfully.
```

```
Contacts in your book:
Name:   Alice,   Phone:   123-456-7890,   Email:
alice@example.com
```

Explanation:

- We created a `ContactBook` class with methods to add, remove, search, and display contacts.
- Each contact is stored in the `contacts` dictionary, with the contact name as the key and another dictionary containing the phone number and email as the value.
- We added two contacts, searched for one, and removed another while displaying the updated contact book.

In this chapter, we explored Python's core data structures—**lists**, **tuples**, **dictionaries**, and **sets**—and learned how to choose the right data structure for the task at hand. We then applied these concepts in a real-world example by creating a simple contact book using Python dictionaries. By understanding and leveraging Python's powerful data structures, you can handle and organize data more effectively, making your applications more efficient and easier to maintain.

Chapter 7: Error Handling and Debugging

One of the most essential skills for a programmer is the ability to handle errors in their code gracefully. In Python, errors are handled using **exceptions**, and you can control what happens when an error occurs using the `try-except` block. This allows you to catch errors and manage them, instead of having the program crash unexpectedly.

1. The `try-except` Block:

- **try block**: The code that might raise an exception is placed inside the `try` block.
- **except block**: If an exception is raised, the program immediately jumps to the `except` block, where you can handle the error.

Example:

```python

try:
```

```
x = 10 / 0     # This will raise a
ZeroDivisionError
except ZeroDivisionError:
    print("Cannot divide by zero!")
```

Explanation:

- The code inside the `try` block attempts to divide 10 by 0, which would normally raise a `ZeroDivisionError`.
- The `except` block catches this specific error and handles it by printing a user-friendly message instead of letting the program crash.

2. Handling Multiple Exceptions:

- You can catch multiple exceptions by using multiple `except` blocks or by catching a general exception using `except Exception`.

Example:

```
python

try:
    value = int(input("Enter a number: "))
    result = 10 / value
except ValueError:
```

```
    print("Invalid input! Please enter a valid
number.")
except ZeroDivisionError.
    print("Cannot divide by zero!")
```

Explanation:

- The `try` block asks for user input and attempts to perform a division. If the user enters something that isn't a number, a `ValueError` is raised. If the user enters 0, a `ZeroDivisionError` is raised. Each exception is handled in its respective `except` block.

3. The `else` and `finally` Blocks:

- The `else` block runs if no exceptions are raised in the `try` block.
- The `finally` block runs regardless of whether an exception was raised or not. It is useful for clean-up actions, such as closing files or releasing resources.

Example:

```python
try:
    x = int(input("Enter a number: "))
    result = 10 / x
```

```
except ValueError:
    print("Please enter a valid number.")
except ZeroDivisionError:
    print("Cannot divide by zero.")
else:
    print(f"The result is {result}")
finally:
    print("Execution completed.")
```

Explanation:

- If no exception occurs, the `else` block will run, displaying the result.

- Regardless of whether there was an exception, the `finally` block will print "Execution completed," making it ideal for clean-up actions.

Raising Exceptions and Debugging Techniques

While Python automatically raises exceptions when errors occur, you can also raise exceptions manually using the `raise` statement. This is useful for defining custom error messages or enforcing certain conditions within your program.

1. Raising Exceptions:

- The `raise` statement allows you to raise exceptions intentionally, either with a specific exception or a custom error message.

Example:

```python
python

def check_age(age):
    if age < 18:
        raise ValueError("Age must be 18 or
older.")
    print("Age is valid.")

try:
    check_age(16)
except ValueError as e:
    print(e)
```

Explanation:

- The `check_age()` function raises a `ValueError` if the age is below 18, and the error message is caught in the `except` block and printed out.

2. Debugging Techniques:

- Debugging is the process of identifying and fixing errors in your code. Python offers several techniques and tools to help you debug efficiently:

  - **Print Statements**: Inserting `print()` statements at various points in your code can help you understand the flow of execution and the state of variables.

  - **The pdb Module**: Python's built-in **debugger** (pdb) allows you to set breakpoints, step through your code, and inspect variable values interactively.

  - **IDEs and Editors**: Many Integrated Development Environments (IDEs), like **PyCharm**, **VS Code**, and **Eclipse**, have built-in debuggers that allow you to set breakpoints and inspect the execution step-by-step.

Example Using pdb:

```python
python

import pdb

def divide(a, b):
    pdb.set_trace()   # Set a breakpoint
    return a / b
```

85

```
print(divide(10, 2))
```

Explanation:

- The `pdb.set_trace()` statement sets a breakpoint, which pauses the program's execution at that point. You can then interact with the program and examine variables to understand what's going wrong.

Real-World Example: Building an App That Validates User Input and Handles Errors

Now that we understand the basics of error handling, let's build a simple Python application that validates user input and handles errors using **try-except** blocks. The app will ask the user to enter their age and ensure it is a valid integer and within a certain range.

Step 1: Write the Function for Input Validation:

- We will use a `while` loop to keep prompting the user until they enter valid input.

```python
def get_user_age():
    while True:
        try:
```

```
        age = int(input("Please enter your
age: "))
        if age < 0 or age > 120:
            raise ValueError("Age must be
between 0 and 120.")
        return age
    except ValueError as e:
        print(f"Error: {e}. Please try
again.")
```

Explanation:

- The function `get_user_age()` asks for input until a valid integer is provided. If the user enters an invalid value or a number outside the range of 0 to 120, a `ValueError` is raised with a custom error message.
- The `while True` loop ensures that the prompt repeats until valid input is given.

Step 2: Call the Function and Handle Errors:

- Now we will call the `get_user_age()` function, which will repeatedly prompt the user for input until the conditions are met.

```python
python
```

87

```
def main():
    print("Welcome to the user age validation
app!")
    age = get_user_age()    # Get valid age from
the user
    print(f"Your age is {age}.")

main()
```

Example Output:

vbnet

```
Welcome to the user age validation app!
Please enter your age: twenty
Error: invalid literal for int() with base 10:
'twenty'. Please try again.
Please enter your age: 150
Error: Age must be between 0 and 120. Please try
again.
Please enter your age: 25
Your age is 25.
```

Explanation:

- If the user enters a non-integer value (like "twenty"), the `ValueError` is caught, and the user is prompted to try again.

- If the user enters an age outside the valid range (e.g., 150), a custom error message is displayed.
- Once valid input is provided, the program prints the user's age.

In this chapter, we've learned the fundamentals of **error handling** in Python using **try-except** blocks, along with techniques for raising exceptions and debugging code. We've also applied these concepts in a real-world example by building a simple app that validates user input and handles errors gracefully.

Effective error handling ensures that your programs are robust and user-friendly by anticipating and managing potential issues. The ability to raise custom exceptions and use debugging tools further improves the development process, allowing you to catch and resolve problems efficiently. As you continue working with Python, mastering error handling and debugging will help you create more reliable and professional applications.

Part 3

Advanced Python Techniques and Libraries

Chapter 8

Exploring Python's Standard Library

An In-Depth Look at Python's Built-In Modules

Python comes with a robust and comprehensive **Standard Library**, which includes a wide range of modules and packages designed to handle common tasks such as file handling, system operations, data manipulation, and more. These modules allow developers to accomplish complex tasks without needing to install third-party packages, making the Standard Library a valuable tool for any Python developer.

In this chapter, we'll explore several of the most commonly used modules in the Python Standard Library, including `os`, `sys`, `datetime`, and others. Understanding how to leverage these built-in tools will help you streamline development and handle cross-platform challenges more efficiently.

1. The `os` Module:

- The os module provides a way to interact with the operating system, allowing you to work with files, directories, and system information.
- It supports a variety of functionalities, such as working with file paths, creating or deleting directories, listing files, and accessing environment variables.

Common Functions in os:

- os.name: Returns the name of the operating system dependent module (e.g., 'posix' for Linux/macOS, 'nt' for Windows).
- os.getcwd(): Returns the current working directory.
- os.listdir(path): Lists the files and directories in the specified path.
- os.mkdir(path): Creates a directory at the specified path.
- os.remove(path): Deletes a file.

Example:

```python

import os

# Get the current working directory
current_directory = os.getcwd()
```

```
print(f"Current Directory: {current_directory}")

# List files in the current directory
files = os.listdir(current_directory)
print(f"Files in current directory: {files}")
```

2. The sys Module:

- The sys module provides access to system-specific parameters and functions. It's particularly useful for interacting with the Python runtime environment and managing input/output operations.
- Key uses of the sys module include managing command-line arguments, handling standard input and output, and exiting programs.

Common Functions in sys:

- sys.argv: A list of command-line arguments passed to the Python script.
- sys.exit(): Exits the program with an optional exit status.
- sys.version: Returns the version of Python currently in use.

Example:

93

```python

import sys

# Print the Python version
print(f"Python version: {sys.version}")

# Print command-line arguments
print(f"Command-line arguments: {sys.argv}")
```

3. The `datetime` Module:

- The `datetime` module provides classes for manipulating dates and times. It's essential for working with time-based data, performing date arithmetic, and formatting dates for display.

- The module supports both **simple** operations (like getting the current date and time) and more **complex** operations (like calculating the difference between two dates).

Common Classes and Functions in `datetime`:

- `datetime.datetime`: Represents both date and time.
- `datetime.date`: Represents the date (year, month, and day).

- `datetime.time`: Represents the time (hours, minutes, seconds).
- `datetime.timedelta`: Represents a time difference between two `datetime` objects.

Example:

python

```
import datetime

# Get the current date and time
now = datetime.datetime.now()
print(f"Current Date and Time: {now}")

# Format the date and time
formatted_now     =      now.strftime("%Y-%m-%d
%H:%M:%S")
print(f"Formatted     Date      and      Time:
{formatted_now}")

# Date arithmetic: calculate the difference
between two dates
today = datetime.date.today()
new_year = datetime.date(2024, 1, 1)
delta = new_year - today
print(f"Days until New Year: {delta.days}")
```

4. Other Useful Modules:

- **`random`**: Provides functions to generate random numbers and perform random operations.
- **`math`**: Provides mathematical functions like trigonometric operations, logarithms, and rounding.
- **`re`**: Provides regular expression matching operations for string manipulation.

Leveraging the Standard Library for Cross-Platform Compatibility

Python's Standard Library is a key asset when building **cross-platform applications**. Since the modules in the Standard Library are designed to be compatible with multiple operating systems, you can write code that works across different platforms without worrying about platform-specific details.

For example:

- The `os` module allows you to handle file paths in a way that works on both **Windows** and **Linux/macOS**. It abstracts the differences in how file paths are handled on each platform, so you don't need to worry about backslashes (\) versus forward slashes (/).
- The `sys` module allows you to handle platform-specific parameters, such as different line endings or Python versions.

- The `datetime` module works uniformly across platforms, allowing you to manipulate dates and times consistently, regardless of the operating system.

By using these modules, you can build Python applications that work seamlessly across different platforms without needing to write platform-specific code.

Real-World Example: Using the `os` Module to Manage Files Across Platforms

Let's build a small application that uses the `os` module to manage files and directories across platforms. This program will:

- Check if a directory exists.
- Create the directory if it doesn't exist.
- List all files in the directory.
- Remove a file from the directory.

Step 1: Write the Program

```python

import os

def manage_files():
```

97

```python
directory = "example_dir"

# Check if the directory exists
if not os.path.exists(directory):
    print(f"Directory '{directory}' does not exist. Creating it now...")
    os.mkdir(directory)     # Create the directory
else:
    print(f"Directory '{directory}' already exists.")

# List files in the directory
print(f"Listing files in '{directory}':")
files = os.listdir(directory)
if files:
    print(files)
else:
    print("No files found in the directory.")

# Create a file in the directory
file_path = os.path.join(directory, "example.txt")
with open(file_path, "w") as file:
    file.write("Hello, world!")
    print(f"File '{file_path}' created and written to.")

# List files again after creating a file
```

```
    files = os.listdir(directory)
    print(f"Files    after    adding    new    file:
{files}")

    # Remove the file
    os.remove(file_path)
    print(f"File '{file_path}' removed.")

# Call the function
manage_files()
```

Explanation:

1. **Directory Checking and Creation**: The program first checks if a directory named `example_dir` exists using `os.path.exists()`. If it doesn't exist, it creates it using `os.mkdir()`.

2. **Listing Files**: The program uses `os.listdir()` to list the files in the directory, displaying them to the user.

3. **File Creation and Writing**: The program creates a file named `example.txt` in the directory and writes a message to it.

4. **File Removal**: The program removes the file using `os.remove()`.

Step 2: Running the Program

When you run the program, the following output will be displayed (assuming the directory example_dir doesn't exist initially):

```vbnet
Directory 'example_dir' does not exist. Creating
it now...
Listing files in 'example_dir':
No files found in the directory.
File    'example_dir/example.txt'    created    and
written to.
Files after adding new file: ['example.txt']
File 'example_dir/example.txt' removed.
```

Cross-Platform Considerations:

- The code will work on **Windows**, **macOS**, and **Linux** without modification, because the os module handles platform-specific file path issues and abstracts them for you.

- On **Windows**, the directory path would use backslashes (\) internally, while on **Linux/macOS**, it would use forward slashes (/), but you don't need to worry about that in the code, as os.path.join() handles this.

In this chapter, we explored Python's **Standard Library**, with an in-depth look at some of the most commonly used modules, such as `os`, `sys`, and `datetime`. We also discussed how the Standard Library supports cross-platform compatibility, making it easier to write Python applications that work seamlessly across different operating systems.

By leveraging the built-in modules provided by Python, you can handle many common tasks—such as working with files, system information, and time-based data—without relying on third-party packages. This makes your applications more efficient, portable, and easier to maintain. In the real-world example, we used the `os` module to manage files across platforms, demonstrating how you can build cross-platform solutions using Python's powerful Standard Library.

Chapter 9

Working with Files and Databases

Reading from and Writing to Files (Text, CSV, JSON)

Handling files is a crucial part of most applications. Python provides built-in functionality to work with various types of files, such as **text files**, **CSV files**, and **JSON files**. In this section, we'll explore how to read from and write to these file formats, and we'll learn how to handle files efficiently in Python.

1. Working with Text Files:

- Text files are the most common type of file you will work with. Python makes it simple to open, read, write, and modify text files using the built-in `open()` function.

Opening a file:

- You can open a file using the `open()` function, which takes two main arguments: the file path and the mode (either for reading, writing, or appending).
- Modes:
  - `'r'`: Read (default mode).
  - `'w'`: Write (creates a new file or overwrites an existing file).
  - `'a'`: Append (adds content to an existing file).

Example:

```python

# Writing to a text file
with open("example.txt", "w") as file:
    file.write("Hello, this is a simple text file.\n")
    file.write("Python makes file handling easy.")

# Reading from a text file
with open("example.txt", "r") as file:
    content = file.read()
    print(content)
```

Explanation:

- The `with open()` statement ensures that the file is properly closed after the block is executed.
- In the first block, we write to the file `example.txt`, and in the second block, we read the content from it.

2. Working with CSV Files:

- CSV (Comma-Separated Values) files are widely used for storing tabular data. Python's **csv module** allows you to read from and write to CSV files easily.

103

Example:

```python
python

import csv

# Writing to a CSV file
data = [["Name", "Age", "City"],
        ["Alice", 30, "New York"],
        ["Bob", 25, "Los Angeles"],
        ["Charlie", 35, "Chicago"]]

with open("people.csv", mode="w", newline="") as
file:
    writer = csv.writer(file)
    writer.writerows(data)

# Reading from a CSV file
with open("people.csv", mode="r") as file:
    reader = csv.reader(file)
    for row in reader:
        print(row)
```

Explanation:

- We first write a list of rows into the CSV file using the `csv.writer()`.
- Then, we read the contents of the CSV file and print each row using the `csv.reader()`.

104

3. Working with JSON Files:

- JSON (JavaScript Object Notation) is a lightweight data-interchange format that is commonly used for exchanging data between a server and a client. Python has a built-in **json module** to parse JSON data.

Example:

```python
import json

# Writing to a JSON file
person = {
    "name": "Alice",
    "age": 30,
    "city": "New York"
}

with open("person.json", "w") as file:
    json.dump(person, file)

# Reading from a JSON file
with open("person.json", "r") as file:
    data = json.load(file)
    print(data)
```

Explanation:

105

- We use `json.dump()` to write Python objects to a JSON file and `json.load()` to read JSON data from a file and convert it back to Python objects.

Introduction to Databases (SQLite, PostgreSQL, MySQL)

While text files and CSV files are useful for storing data, databases provide a more powerful and efficient way to store, retrieve, and manipulate large amounts of data. Python provides libraries for interacting with various database systems, including **SQLite**, **PostgreSQL**, and **MySQL**.

1. SQLite:

- **SQLite** is a lightweight, serverless relational database engine that stores data in a single file. Python's `sqlite3` module provides a simple API for interacting with SQLite databases.

Example:

```python
python

import sqlite3

# Connect to SQLite database (or create it if it
doesn't exist)
conn = sqlite3.connect('example.db')
```

```python
cursor = conn.cursor()

# Create a table
cursor.execute('''CREATE   TABLE   IF   NOT   EXISTS
users
                  (id  INTEGER  PRIMARY  KEY,  name
TEXT, age INTEGER)''')

# Insert data into the table
cursor.execute("INSERT   INTO   users   (name,   age)
VALUES ('Alice', 30)")
cursor.execute("INSERT   INTO   users   (name,   age)
VALUES ('Bob', 25)")

# Commit the changes
conn.commit()

# Retrieve data from the table
cursor.execute("SELECT * FROM users")
rows = cursor.fetchall()

for row in rows:
    print(row)

# Close the connection
conn.close()
```

Explanation:

- We connect to an SQLite database and create a table to store user information.
- Then, we insert data into the table and retrieve it using `SELECT`.

2. PostgreSQL and MySQL:

- **PostgreSQL** and **MySQL** are full-fledged relational database management systems (RDBMS) commonly used in production environments.
- Python provides libraries like **psycopg2** (for PostgreSQL) and **mysql-connector-python** (for MySQL) to interact with these databases.

To use these databases in Python:

- Install the appropriate library using `pip`:

```bash
bash

pip install psycopg2   # For PostgreSQL
pip install mysql-connector-python   # For MySQL
```

- Use similar approaches as with SQLite: connect to the database, execute queries, and fetch results.

Real-World Example: Building a Simple Note-Taking App that Stores Data in a Database

Now, let's build a simple note-taking app using Python and SQLite. The app will allow users to create, view, and delete notes. We will store these notes in an SQLite database.

Step 1: Define the Database Schema

- We'll create a table called `notes` to store the title and content of each note.

python

```
import sqlite3

def create_table():
    conn = sqlite3.connect('notes.db')
    cursor = conn.cursor()
    cursor.execute('''CREATE TABLE IF NOT EXISTS
notes
                    (id INTEGER PRIMARY KEY,
title TEXT, content TEXT)''')
    conn.commit()
    conn.close()
```

Step 2: Add a Note

- This function will insert a new note into the database.

```python
python


def add_note(title, content):
    conn = sqlite3.connect('notes.db')
    cursor = conn.cursor()
    cursor.execute("INSERT  INTO  notes  (title,
content) VALUES (?, ?)", (title, content))
    conn.commit()
    conn.close()
    print("Note added successfully!")
```

Step 3: View All Notes

- This function will retrieve and display all notes from the database.

```python
python


def view_notes():
    conn = sqlite3.connect('notes.db')
    cursor = conn.cursor()
    cursor.execute("SELECT * FROM notes")
    rows = cursor.fetchall()
    if rows:
        for row in rows:
            print(f"ID:    {row[0]},    Title:
{row[1]}, Content: {row[2]}")
    else:
        print("No notes available.")
```

110

```
conn.close()
```

Step 4: Delete a Note

- This function will delete a note based on its ID.

python

```python
def delete_note(note_id):
    conn = sqlite3.connect('notes.db')
    cursor = conn.cursor()
    cursor.execute("DELETE FROM notes WHERE id =
?", (note_id,))
    conn.commit()
    conn.close()
    print("Note deleted successfully!")
```

Step 5: Putting It All Together

Now, we will build a simple interface to interact with the user.

python

```python
def main():
    create_table()

    while True:
```

111

```python
        print("\n1. Add Note\n2. View Notes\n3.
Delete Note\n4. Exit")
        choice = input("Enter your choice: ")

        if choice == '1':
            title = input("Enter note title: ")
            content = input("Enter note content:
")
            add_note(title, content)
        elif choice == '2':
            view_notes()
        elif choice == '3':
            note_id = int(input("Enter note ID to
delete: "))
            delete_note(note_id)
        elif choice == '4':
            break
        else:
            print("Invalid   choice.   Please   try
again.")

if __name__ == "__main__":
    main()
```

Explanation:

- The program starts by creating the notes table if it doesn't already exist.

- The user is presented with a menu to add, view, or delete notes.
- Notes are stored in an SQLite database, and the program interacts with the database to perform the desired operations.

Example Output:

```
pgsql

1. Add Note
2. View Notes
3. Delete Note
4. Exit
Enter your choice: 1
Enter note title: Python Basics
Enter note content: Learn the basics of Python
programming.

Note added successfully!

1. Add Note
2. View Notes
3. Delete Note
4. Exit
Enter your choice: 2
ID: 1, Title: Python Basics, Content: Learn the
basics of Python programming.
```

```
1. Add Note
2. View Notes
3. Delete Note
4. Exit
Enter your choice: 3
Enter note ID to delete: 1
Note deleted successfully!
```

In this chapter, we explored how to work with files and databases in Python. We covered how to read from and write to text, CSV, and JSON files using Python's built-in modules. We also introduced databases like **SQLite**, **PostgreSQL**, and **MySQL**, explaining how to interact with them using Python.

We then applied this knowledge to build a real-world **note-taking app** that uses an SQLite database to store, retrieve, and delete notes. By using the powerful libraries Python provides for file and database handling, you can create more robust and scalable applications that store and manage data efficiently.

Chapter 10

Python for Networking and Web Development

Basics of Sockets, HTTP Requests, and APIs

Python is widely used in **networking** and **web development**, thanks to its powerful libraries that make handling sockets, HTTP requests, and APIs straightforward. Understanding these fundamental concepts is essential for building networked applications, web services, and interacting with third-party services.

1. Sockets:

- **Sockets** provide the fundamental technology for communication between computers over a network. They are used to establish connections, send data, and receive data between client and server applications.
- Python's `socket` module allows you to work with sockets, enabling you to create both **client** and **server** applications that can communicate over the network.

Example of Creating a Simple Server:

115

```python
python

import socket

# Create a socket object
server_socket    =    socket.socket(socket.AF_INET,
socket.SOCK_STREAM)

# Bind the socket to a specific address and port
server_socket.bind(("localhost", 8080))

# Listen for incoming connections
server_socket.listen(5)
print("Server listening on port 8080...")

# Accept incoming connections
client_socket,         client_address          =
server_socket.accept()
print(f"Connection    from    {client_address}
established!")

# Send a message to the client
client_socket.sendall(b"Hello from the server!")

# Close the connection
client_socket.close()
```

Explanation:

- This code sets up a simple **TCP server** that listens on port 8080. It accepts a connection from a client, sends a message, and then closes the connection.

2. HTTP Requests and APIs:

- **HTTP requests** are used to interact with web servers, retrieving data or sending data. The most common HTTP methods include:
  - GET: Retrieve data from a server.
  - POST: Send data to a server.
  - PUT: Update data on the server.
  - DELETE: Remove data from the server.
- **APIs (Application Programming Interfaces)** allow applications to interact with each other over the web. APIs typically expose **RESTful** endpoints for easy integration with other services.

Python's `requests` library is a simple, yet powerful tool for making HTTP requests and interacting with APIs.

Example of Making an HTTP GET Request:

```python
import requests
```

```
# Sending a GET request to a public API
response                                    =
requests.get("https://jsonplaceholder.typicode.
com/todos/1")

# Print the response in JSON format
print(response.json())
```

Explanation:

- The code sends a GET request to a public API that returns a to-do item in JSON format. The response is then parsed using .json().

Using Python for Cross-Platform Web Development with Flask and Django

Python is an excellent language for **web development**, offering frameworks like **Flask** and **Django** for building scalable and maintainable web applications.

1. Flask:

- **Flask** is a lightweight, micro-framework for building web applications. It's flexible and simple to use, making it a great choice for small to medium-sized projects, RESTful APIs, and microservices.

- Flask allows you to quickly set up routes (URLs), define HTTP methods (e.g., GET, POST), and handle responses.

Basic Flask Example:

```python
from flask import Flask, jsonify

app = Flask(__name__)

@app.route('/')
def hello_world():
    return 'Hello, World!'

@app.route('/api')
def api():
    return jsonify(message="Hello from the API")

if __name__ == '__main__':
    app.run(debug=True)
```

Explanation:

- This Flask application defines two routes: a simple hello_world() function that returns a message, and an /api route that returns a JSON response.

2. Django:

- **Django** is a high-level web framework that follows the **Model-View-Controller (MVC)** pattern. It's more feature-rich than Flask, providing built-in functionalities like authentication, form handling, and database management, making it a great choice for larger projects.
- Django has an **admin panel** for managing database content, a powerful ORM (Object-Relational Mapping) system, and many other built-in utilities.

Basic Django Example:

- Setting up a Django project involves installing Django, creating a project, and running a development server. This involves more setup than Flask, but it offers more built-in features.

bash

```
# Install Django
pip install django

# Create a new Django project
django-admin startproject mysite

# Create an app
cd mysite
python manage.py startapp myapp
```

```
# Run the development server
python manage.py runserver
```

Explanation:

- Once the server is running, you can create routes in the `views.py` file within the `myapp` folder, and map them to URLs using Django's `urls.py`.

Real-World Example: Building a REST API with Flask for a Simple Task Manager

In this real-world example, we will build a **simple task manager** REST API using **Flask**. The API will allow users to:

- Create a task.
- View all tasks.
- Update a task.
- Delete a task.

Step 1: Set Up Flask Application

```python
from flask import Flask, request, jsonify

app = Flask(__name__)
```

```python
# In-memory storage for tasks
tasks = []

# Route to create a task
@app.route('/tasks', methods=['POST'])
def create_task():
    data = request.get_json()
    task = {
        'id': len(tasks) + 1,
        'title': data['title'],
        'done': False
    }
    tasks.append(task)
    return jsonify(task), 201

# Route to get all tasks
@app.route('/tasks', methods=['GET'])
def get_tasks():
    return jsonify(tasks)

# Route to update a task
@app.route('/tasks/<int:task_id>',
methods=['PUT'])
def update_task(task_id):
    task = next((t for t in tasks if t['id'] ==
task_id), None)
    if task is None:
```

122

```
        return   jsonify({'error':   'Task   not
found'}), 404

    data = request.get_json()
    task['title']        =        data.get('title',
task['title'])
    task['done']         =         data.get('done',
task['done'])

    return jsonify(task)

# Route to delete a task
@app.route('/tasks/<int:task_id>',
methods=['DELETE'])
def delete_task(task_id):
    task = next((t for t in tasks if t['id'] ==
task_id), None)
    if task is None:
        return   jsonify({'error':   'Task   not
found'}), 404

    tasks.remove(task)
    return '', 204

if __name__ == '__main__':
    app.run(debug=True)
```

Explanation:

- We define a list called `tasks` to store our task data in memory.
- The `/tasks` route allows clients to create new tasks via the `POST` method and retrieve all tasks via the `GET` method.
- The `/tasks/<int:task_id>` route allows updating or deleting a task based on its `id`.

Step 2: Testing the API with HTTP Requests

Now that our API is set up, we can test it using `curl`, Postman, or Python's `requests` library.

Creating a Task:

bash

```
curl -X POST -H "Content-Type: application/json"
-d      '{"title":      "Learn      Flask"}'
http://localhost:5000/tasks
```

Updating a Task:

bash

```
curl -X PUT -H "Content-Type: application/json"
-d '{"title": "Learn Flask and Python", "done":
true}' http://localhost:5000/tasks/1
```

124

Viewing All Tasks:

bash

```
curl http://localhost:5000/tasks
```

Deleting a Task:

bash

```
curl -X DELETE http://localhost:5000/tasks/1
```

Example Output:

arduino

```
Task Created:
{
  "id": 1,
  "title": "Learn Flask",
  "done": false
}


Task Updated:
{
  "id": 1,
  "title": "Learn Flask and Python",
  "done": true
}
```

125

```
All Tasks:
[
  {
    "id": 1,
    "title": "Learn Flask and Python",
    "done": true
  }
]


Task Deleted: (No content, HTTP status 204)
```

In this chapter, we learned about Python's capabilities for **networking** and **web development**. We explored how to work with **sockets**, make **HTTP requests**, and interact with **APIs**. Additionally, we learned how to use **Flask** for building cross-platform web applications and APIs.

Finally, we applied these concepts by building a **REST API** for a simple task manager app using **Flask**, where we implemented functionality to create, view, update, and delete tasks. Understanding networking and web development concepts in Python opens up numerous possibilities for building powerful, scalable web applications and services.

Whether you're building a small API or a large web application, Python's simplicity and the power of

126

frameworks like Flask and Django make it an excellent choice for web development.

Chapter 11

Multi-Threading and Concurrency in Python

Understanding Threading, Multiprocessing, and Asynchronous Programming

Concurrency is the ability to run multiple tasks or processes simultaneously. This is a critical aspect of software development, especially for improving the performance of programs that need to perform I/O-bound tasks (like downloading files, reading from a database, etc.). Python provides several techniques to handle concurrency, including **threading, multiprocessing**, and **asynchronous programming**.

1. Threading:

- **Threading** allows you to run multiple threads (smaller units of a process) concurrently within the same process. Each thread has its own local memory, but shares the global memory of the process.
- Python provides the `threading` module to create and manage threads. However, Python's **Global Interpreter**

128

Lock (GIL) restricts the simultaneous execution of multiple threads on multiple cores in CPython (the standard Python implementation). This means threading is generally more beneficial for I/O-bound tasks rather than CPU-bound tasks.

Example of Threading:

```python
python

import threading
import time

def print_numbers():
    for i in range(5):
        time.sleep(1)
        print(i)

def print_letters():
    for letter in 'abcde':
        time.sleep(1.5)
        print(letter)

# Create threads
thread1 = threading.Thread(target=print_numbers)
thread2 = threading.Thread(target=print_letters)

# Start threads
thread1.start()
```

```
thread2.start()

# Wait for both threads to complete
thread1.join()
thread2.join()

print("Finished!")
```

Explanation:

- Two threads are created to run `print_numbers()` and `print_letters()`.
- Each thread runs concurrently, and we use `join()` to ensure that the main program waits for the threads to complete before exiting.

2. Multiprocessing:

- **Multiprocessing** involves creating separate processes, each with its own memory space. This approach is beneficial for CPU-bound tasks, as each process runs in parallel and can take advantage of multiple CPU cores.
- Python's `multiprocessing` module allows you to create processes, and it avoids the limitations of the GIL by running each process independently.

Example of Multiprocessing:

```python
python

import multiprocessing
import time

def square(number):
    time.sleep(1)
    print(f"The    square    of    {number}    is
{number**2}")

if __name__ == '__main__':
    # Create processes
    process1                                    =
multiprocessing.Process(target=square,
args=(2,))
    process2                                    =
multiprocessing.Process(target=square,
args=(3,))

    # Start processes
    process1.start()
    process2.start()

    # Wait for processes to complete
    process1.join()
    process2.join()

    print("Finished!")
```

Explanation:

131

- This example uses the `multiprocessing` module to run two processes concurrently. Each process computes the square of a number independently and in parallel.

3. Asynchronous Programming:

- **Asynchronous programming** allows a program to run code concurrently without using threads or processes. It is especially useful for I/O-bound tasks (like web scraping, downloading files, or querying a database).
- In Python, you can use **asyncio**, the built-in library for writing asynchronous programs. With `async` and `await`, you can run tasks concurrently without blocking the main thread.

Example of Asynchronous Programming:

```python
import asyncio

async def download_file(file_id):
    print(f"Downloading file {file_id}...")
    await asyncio.sleep(2)   # Simulating file
download
    print(f"File {file_id} downloaded!")

async def main():
```

132

```
    tasks = [download_file(1), download_file(2),
download_file(3)]
    await asyncio.gather(*tasks)

asyncio.run(main())
```

Explanation:

- The `download_file()` function is asynchronous, allowing it to simulate downloading a file without blocking the program.
- The `asyncio.gather()` function is used to run multiple tasks concurrently, and `await` is used to pause the program until a task completes.

How to Manage Concurrency Across Platforms with Python

Managing concurrency across different platforms is essential when your program needs to run on multiple operating systems, such as **Windows**, **macOS**, and **Linux**. Fortunately, Python's concurrency mechanisms—whether threading, multiprocessing, or asyncio—are cross-platform and can be used on any major OS.

- **Threading and Multiprocessing**: Both `threading` and `multiprocessing` are supported on **Windows**, **macOS**, and **Linux**. However, keep in mind that multiprocessing

133

will work best on systems that support multiple CPU cores, allowing processes to run concurrently on separate CPUs.

- **Asynchronous Programming**: Asynchronous programming with `asyncio` is also platform-agnostic. The asyncio event loop works consistently across platforms and is an excellent choice for I/O-bound tasks.

When developing cross-platform Python applications, you should consider the task's nature—whether it is I/O-bound (best suited for `asyncio` or `threading`) or CPU-bound (best suited for `multiprocessing`). Additionally, ensure you handle any platform-specific issues (e.g., file system differences, networking restrictions) appropriately.

Real-World Example: Creating a Python Application That Downloads Multiple Files Concurrently

Let's now build a simple application that downloads multiple files concurrently using **asynchronous programming**. The program will simulate downloading files using `asyncio` and `aiohttp` (a library for asynchronous HTTP requests).

Step 1: Install `aiohttp` Library:

```bash
bash

pip install aiohttp
```

Step 2: Create the Asynchronous File Download Application:

```python
python

import asyncio
import aiohttp

async def download_file(url, session):
    print(f"Start downloading: {url}")
    async with session.get(url) as response:
        content = await response.read()
        print(f"Finished    downloading:    {url}
(Content length: {len(content)} bytes)")

async def main():
    urls = [
        "https://www.example.com/file1.txt",
        "https://www.example.com/file2.txt",
        "https://www.example.com/file3.txt"
    ]

    async with aiohttp.ClientSession() as session:
```

```
        tasks = [download_file(url, session) for
url in urls]
        await asyncio.gather(*tasks)

# Run the program
asyncio.run(main())
```

Explanation:

- The `download_file()` function simulates downloading a file from a URL asynchronously.
- We use the `aiohttp` library to handle the HTTP requests asynchronously, allowing multiple files to be downloaded concurrently.
- The `asyncio.gather()` function gathers all download tasks and runs them concurrently.

Example Output:

```perl
Start                          downloading:
https://www.example.com/file1.txt
Start                          downloading:
https://www.example.com/file2.txt
Start                          downloading:
https://www.example.com/file3.txt
```

```
Finished                        downloading:
https://www.example.com/file1.txt      (Content
length: 12345 bytes)
Finished                        downloading:
https://www.example.com/file2.txt      (Content
length: 67890 bytes)
Finished                        downloading:
https://www.example.com/file3.txt      (Content
length: 112233 bytes)
```

Explanation of the Output:

- The program downloads three files concurrently, printing a message when each download starts and finishes.
- Since the downloads happen concurrently, the output shows that all downloads occur in parallel, and the total time taken is reduced compared to sequential downloads.

In this chapter, we covered the key concepts of **threading**, **multiprocessing**, and **asynchronous programming** in Python. We discussed how these approaches differ in terms of concurrency management, and how you can use them to handle I/O-bound or CPU-bound tasks effectively.

- **Threading** is useful for tasks that are I/O-bound and require concurrent operations within the same process.
- **Multiprocessing** is ideal for CPU-bound tasks, allowing processes to run independently on separate cores.
- **Asynchronous programming** using `asyncio` is the most efficient way to handle I/O-bound tasks without blocking the main thread.

We also built a real-world example of a Python application that downloads multiple files concurrently using **asynchronous programming**. Understanding these concurrency models will help you write more efficient Python programs, particularly when dealing with tasks that require high levels of parallelism.

Chapter 12

Python for Automation and Scripting

Automating Tasks with Python Scripts

Automation is one of Python's most powerful use cases. Python scripts can save time and reduce manual errors by automating repetitive tasks. Whether it's automating web scraping, posting on social media, or managing system processes, Python's simplicity and wide array of libraries make it an ideal choice for automation tasks.

In this chapter, we will explore how Python can be used to automate common tasks. We'll look at using Python for **web automation**, **web scraping**, and **system automation**, and how Python libraries like `selenium`, `requests`, and `pyautogui` can help us automate tasks across different platforms.

1. Automating Tasks with Python Scripts:

- Python scripts can automate a wide range of tasks. A script might involve reading data from a file, making HTTP requests to a server, interacting with web pages, or performing system operations like renaming files or sending emails.

- For example, Python can automate tasks like:
    - Data extraction and manipulation.
    - File system management.
    - Web scraping.
    - Sending emails or alerts.
    - Interacting with web applications (using automation tools like `selenium`).

Using Libraries Like Selenium, Requests, and PyAutoGUI for Cross-Platform Automation

Python's **standard library** and **third-party libraries** provide powerful tools for automating tasks across different platforms (Windows, macOS, Linux). Below, we will explore some commonly used libraries for automation.

1. Selenium for Web Automation:

- **Selenium** is a powerful tool used for automating web browsers. It allows you to control a browser instance (such as Chrome or Firefox) and interact with web pages programmatically, making it perfect for tasks like testing web applications or automating repetitive browser actions.

Common Use Cases:

- Filling out forms on websites.
- Clicking buttons or navigating through pages.
- Extracting data from websites (web scraping).
- Automating logins and other user interactions.

Example: Automating a Google Search with Selenium:

First, you need to install Selenium and a WebDriver (e.g., ChromeDriver for Chrome).

```bash
pip install selenium
```

Script to automate Google search:

```python
from selenium import webdriver
from selenium.webdriver.common.keys import Keys

# Set up WebDriver (you need to have ChromeDriver
installed)
```

```python
driver                                        =
webdriver.Chrome(executable_path="/path/to/chro
medriver")

# Open Google
driver.get("https://www.google.com")

# Find the search box, type a query, and hit Enter
search_box = driver.find_element("name", "q")
search_box.send_keys("Python    automation    with
Selenium")
search_box.send_keys(Keys.RETURN)

# Wait for a few seconds for the results to load
driver.implicitly_wait(5)

# Print the title of the page
print(driver.title)

# Close the browser window
driver.quit()
```

Explanation:

- This script opens a Chrome browser, navigates to Google, performs a search, and prints the page title. Selenium allows for complex interactions like scrolling, clicking, and form filling.

2. Requests for Web Scraping and HTTP Automation:

- **Requests** is a simple and easy-to-use library for making HTTP requests in Python. It is widely used for web scraping and interacting with APIs to automate tasks like data retrieval, sending data, and posting on websites.

Common Use Cases:

- Fetching data from APIs.
- Web scraping (retrieving and parsing web page content).
- Automating form submissions and posting data to servers.

Example: Web Scraping with Requests:

```python
python

import requests
from bs4 import BeautifulSoup

# Send a GET request to a website
response = requests.get("https://example.com")
response.raise_for_status()    # Check if the request was successful

# Parse the HTML content with BeautifulSoup
```

143

```
soup        =        BeautifulSoup(response.text,
'html.parser')

# Extract all links (anchor tags) from the
webpage
links = soup.find_all('a')
for link in links:
    print(link.get('href'))
```

Explanation:

- This script uses `requests` to fetch the HTML content from a webpage and then parses it with `BeautifulSoup`. It extracts all the links (<a> tags) from the page.

3. PyAutoGUI for GUI Automation:

- **PyAutoGUI** is a cross-platform library that allows you to automate GUI interactions like mouse movements, clicks, keyboard input, and screen capture.
- It's useful for automating tasks on your computer that involve interacting with the graphical user interface (GUI), such as filling out forms, clicking buttons, or navigating through different windows.

Common Use Cases:

144

- Automating repetitive GUI tasks (e.g., filling out forms or clicking buttons).
- Simulating keyboard or mouse input.
- Automating game controls or office software.

Example: Automating Mouse and Keyboard with PyAutoGUI:

bash

```
pip install pyautogui
```

Script to move the mouse and click:

python

```
import pyautogui
import time

# Move the mouse to a specific position (x=100,
y=200)
pyautogui.moveTo(100, 200, duration=1)

# Click the mouse at the current position
pyautogui.click()

# Type text using the keyboard
pyautogui.write('Hello, world!', interval=0.1)
```

145

```
# Press the 'enter' key
pyautogui.press('enter')


# Take a screenshot
pyautogui.screenshot('screenshot.png')
```

Explanation:

- This script moves the mouse to a specific location on the screen, clicks, types text, presses the Enter key, and takes a screenshot of the screen.

Real-World Example: Automating Social Media Posting or Web Scraping Tasks

Now, let's put everything together with a **real-world example**. In this case, we will automate the process of posting to **Twitter** using Python. We'll use **Tweepy** (a Python library for the Twitter API) for social media automation and **requests** for web scraping tasks.

Step 1: Install Tweepy and Requests:

bash

```
pip install tweepy requests
```

146

Step 2: Automating Twitter Posting with Tweepy: To use **Tweepy**, you need to create a Twitter Developer account and obtain API keys. After getting the keys, you can authenticate and post to Twitter using Python.

```python
import tweepy

# Authentication credentials (replace with your
own API keys)
consumer_key = 'your_consumer_key'
consumer_secret = 'your_consumer_secret'
access_token = 'your_access_token'
access_token_secret = 'your_access_token_secret'

# Authenticate to Twitter
auth       =       tweepy.OAuthHandler(consumer_key,
consumer_secret)
auth.set_access_token(access_token,
access_token_secret)

# Create an API object
api = tweepy.API(auth)

# Post a tweet
api.update_status("Hello,  world!  This  is  an
automated tweet from Python.")
```

147

Explanation:

- This script authenticates with Twitter using your API keys and posts a simple tweet. The `update_status()` method is used to send the tweet.

Step 3: Automating Web Scraping with Requests: Let's scrape a website to get a list of trending articles, then post them to Twitter.

```python
python


import requests
from bs4 import BeautifulSoup
import tweepy


# Get trending articles from a blog or news site
response = requests.get("https://example.com")
soup        =        BeautifulSoup(response.text,
'html.parser')


# Extract titles of articles (assuming articles
are in <h2> tags)
articles = soup.find_all('h2')
article_titles = [article.text for article in
articles]


# Post each article title to Twitter
for title in article_titles:
```

148

```
api.update_status(f"Check out this article:
{title}")
```

Explanation:

- The script fetches a webpage and scrapes the titles of articles (assuming the titles are in <h2> tags). Each article title is then posted as a tweet using Tweepy.

In this chapter, we explored how Python can be used for **automation** and **scripting**. We covered several useful libraries, such as **Selenium** for web automation, **Requests** for web scraping, and **PyAutoGUI** for GUI automation. By leveraging these libraries, you can automate a wide range of tasks across different platforms.

We also implemented a **real-world example** of automating social media posting and web scraping tasks. Automation with Python not only saves time but also helps reduce human error, making it a valuable tool for developers and businesses alike.

Part 4

Cross-Platform Tools and Techniques

Chapter 13

Introduction to Cross-Platform Development Tools

Overview of Cross-Platform Development Frameworks

In modern software development, the ability to build applications that run seamlessly across multiple platforms is a key factor for success. Cross-platform development frameworks enable developers to write code once and deploy it on **Windows**, **macOS**, **Linux**, and even **mobile platforms** like **Android** and **iOS**.

Python, with its wide range of libraries and frameworks, is well-suited for building cross-platform applications. These tools handle platform-specific details (such as GUI rendering and file handling), allowing developers to focus on the core functionality of their applications without worrying about platform differences.

In this chapter, we will explore some of the most popular cross-platform development frameworks for Python, including **PyInstaller**, **Kivy**, **Qt**, and **Electron**.

How Tools Like PyInstaller, Kivy, Qt, and Electron Help Python Developers Build Cross-Platform Apps

1. PyInstaller:

- **PyInstaller** is a tool that allows you to package Python applications into standalone executables. It supports cross-platform development by bundling the Python interpreter and dependencies into a single executable file, eliminating the need for users to install Python or any dependencies.
- **Common Use Cases**:
    - Creating cross-platform executables for desktop applications.
    - Distributing Python applications without requiring a Python installation.
- **Supported Platforms**:
    - **Windows, macOS, Linux**.

Example (Basic PyInstaller usage):

bash

```
# Package a Python script into an executable
pyinstaller my_script.py
```

Explanation:

- After running this command, PyInstaller creates an executable file in the `dist/` directory, which can be run on the target platform without requiring a separate Python environment.

2. Kivy:

- **Kivy** is a powerful, open-source Python framework for developing multi-touch applications, including graphical user interfaces (GUIs). It allows you to create cross-platform applications that can run on **Windows**, **macOS**, **Linux**, **Android**, and **iOS**.
- **Common Use Cases**:
  - Building mobile and desktop applications with graphical interfaces.
  - Creating applications that involve multi-touch input and other gesture-based interactions.
- **Supported Platforms**:
  - **Windows**, **macOS**, **Linux**, **Android**, **iOS**.

Example (Creating a simple Kivy app):

```python
from kivy.app import App
from kivy.uix.button import Button
```

```
class MyApp(App):
    def build(self):
        return Button(text="Hello, Kivy!")

if __name__ == "__main__":
    MyApp().run()
```

Explanation:

- This simple Kivy app creates a button that says "Hello, Kivy!" when run. The application is cross-platform, meaning it will run on any of the supported platforms without modification.

3. Qt (PyQt5):

- **PyQt** is a set of Python bindings for the **Qt** application framework, which is widely used for creating desktop applications with graphical interfaces. PyQt provides tools for building feature-rich, native-looking cross-platform applications.
- **Common Use Cases:**
  - Building desktop applications with rich UIs.
  - Creating applications that require high performance and native OS look and feel.
- **Supported Platforms:**
  - **Windows, macOS, Linux.**

Example (Simple PyQt5 app):

python

```python
import sys
from PyQt5.QtWidgets import QApplication,
QWidget, QPushButton

class MyApp(QWidget):
    def __init__(self):
        super().__init__()
        self.setWindowTitle('PyQt5 App')
        self.setGeometry(100, 100, 300, 200)
        button = QPushButton('Click Me!', self)
        button.clicked.connect(self.on_click)
        button.resize(button.sizeHint())
        button.move(100, 80)

    def on_click(self):
        print("Button clicked!")

if __name__ == '__main__':
    app = QApplication(sys.argv)
    window = MyApp()
    window.show()
    sys.exit(app.exec_())
```

Explanation:

155

- This PyQt5 application creates a window with a button that, when clicked, prints "Button clicked!" to the console. PyQt is widely used for creating feature-rich desktop applications.

4. Electron:

- **Electron** is a popular framework for building cross-platform desktop applications using **web technologies** (HTML, CSS, JavaScript). While Electron itself is not a Python framework, Python developers can use Electron in combination with Python backend services to build desktop applications.
- **Common Use Cases**:
    o Building desktop applications with web-based UIs.
    o Creating apps that need to interact with Python backends for data processing or logic.
- **Supported Platforms**:
    o **Windows, macOS, Linux**.

Explanation:

- Electron allows you to create desktop applications with a web-like interface. Python can be used in the backend for processing or interacting with APIs, while the frontend (UI) can be built using HTML, CSS, and JavaScript.

Real-World Example: Setting Up a Basic Cross-Platform GUI App with Kivy

Now, let's build a simple **cross-platform GUI app** using **Kivy**. This app will have a button that, when clicked, displays a message.

Step 1: Install Kivy

bash

```
pip install kivy
```

Step 2: Create the Kivy Application

python

```
from kivy.app import App
from kivy.uix.button import Button
from kivy.uix.label import Label
from kivy.uix.boxlayout import BoxLayout

class MyApp(App):
    def build(self):
```

```
        layout                                    =
BoxLayout(orientation='vertical')

        # Create a button
        self.button = Button(text="Click me!")

self.button.bind(on_press=self.on_button_click)

        # Create a label
        self.label = Label(text="Hello, Kivy!")

        # Add the button and label to the layout
        layout.add_widget(self.button)
        layout.add_widget(self.label)

        return layout

    def on_button_click(self, instance):
        self.label.text = "Button clicked!"

if __name__ == "__main__":
    MyApp().run()
```

Explanation:

- We define a class `MyApp` that inherits from `App`, which is the base class for all Kivy applications.

- The app contains a `Button` and a `Label`. When the button is pressed, the `on_button_click()` method is called, changing the text of the label.
- The `BoxLayout` is used to arrange the button and label vertically.

Step 3: Running the Application

- To run this app, simply save the code to a file (e.g., `main.py`), and run it using Python:

```bash
python main.py
```

Step 4: Packaging the Application for Cross-Platform Use

- You can package this Kivy app into a standalone executable using **PyInstaller** or **Buildozer** (for mobile platforms like Android and iOS).
  - To package the app for desktop, install **PyInstaller**:

```bash
pip install pyinstaller
```

159

- o Then, run:

```bash
bash

pyinstaller --onefile main.py
```

- o This will create an executable that can be run on the target platform without needing Python installed.

In this chapter, we explored various **cross-platform development frameworks** that help Python developers build applications that run on multiple platforms. These include:

- **PyInstaller**: A tool for packaging Python scripts into standalone executables.
- **Kivy**: A framework for building cross-platform mobile and desktop applications with graphical interfaces.
- **PyQt5**: A set of Python bindings for the Qt framework, enabling the creation of native desktop applications.
- **Electron**: A framework for building cross-platform desktop applications using web technologies, which can be integrated with Python for backend processing.

160

We also built a simple **Kivy-based GUI app** that demonstrates how to use Python for cross-platform development. With these tools, Python developers can easily create applications that work across different operating systems, enabling them to reach a wider audience and simplify the development process. Whether you're building a desktop app, mobile app, or command-line tool, these cross-platform frameworks provide the flexibility to bring your ideas to life efficiently.

Chapter 14

Building Cross-Platform Command-Line Tools

Creating Command-Line Tools with Python That Work Across Different Platforms

Command-line tools are an essential part of many systems, providing efficient ways to interact with software without the need for graphical user interfaces (GUIs). Python, being a versatile and platform-independent language, makes it easy to create cross-platform command-line tools that can be used on **Windows**, **macOS**, and **Linux**.

Python provides several modules to handle common tasks in command-line tool development, such as parsing arguments, handling file I/O, and executing system commands. Two popular libraries for building user-friendly and flexible command-line tools are `argparse` and `click`.

In this chapter, we will explore how to create command-line tools with Python, and how to use `argparse` and `click` to manage command-line arguments and options. Finally, we

162

will implement a real-world example of a command-line tool that manages system tasks, like file management and process handling.

Using argparse and click for Command-Line Arguments and Options

1. argparse Module:

- **argparse** is a built-in Python module that makes it easy to write user-friendly command-line interfaces. It allows you to specify what command-line options the program accepts, parse the command-line arguments, and generate help messages.

- You can use argparse to define positional arguments (required), optional arguments, and even subcommands for more complex tools.

Basic Example with argparse:

```python
import argparse

# Create the parser
parser = argparse.ArgumentParser(description="A simple command-line tool.")
```

163

```python
# Define command-line arguments
parser.add_argument('name', type=str, help="Your
name")
parser.add_argument('-a',    '--age',    type=int,
help="Your age", default=25)

# Parse the arguments
args = parser.parse_args()

# Use the arguments
print(f"Hello, {args.name}!")
print(f"You are {args.age} years old.")
```

Explanation:

- In this example, we define two arguments:
  - name (positional argument): The user must provide their name.
  - -a or --age (optional argument): The user can specify their age, with a default value of 25 if not provided.
- We use args to access the values of the arguments and print them.

Running the script:

```bash
bash
```

164

```
python script.py Alice --age 30
```

Output:

```
sql
```

```
Hello, Alice!
You are 30 years old.
```

2. click Library:

- click is another popular Python library for building command-line interfaces. It provides an easier and more flexible way to handle command-line arguments, options, and commands. Unlike argparse, click uses decorators to define arguments and commands, making the code cleaner and more Pythonic.

Basic Example with click:

```
python
```

```
import click
```

```
@click.command()
@click.argument('name')
@click.option('--age', default=25, help="Your age")
```

165

```
def greet(name, age):
    click.echo(f"Hello, {name}!")
    click.echo(f"You are {age} years old.")

if __name__ == '__main__':
    greet()
```

Explanation:

- We define a command `greet` using the `@click.command()` decorator.
- The `@click.argument()` decorator is used to define required arguments, while `@click.option()` is used for optional arguments.
- The `click.echo()` function is used for printing output in a way that works consistently across platforms.

Running the script:

```
bash
```

```
python script.py Alice --age 30
```

Output:

```
sql
```

```
Hello, Alice!
You are 30 years old.
```

Real-World Example: Developing a Command-Line Tool to Manage System Tasks

Let's build a simple **command-line tool** that automates basic **system tasks**, such as:

- Listing files in a directory.
- Creating new directories.
- Deleting files.

We'll use `argparse` for this example, but you could easily switch to `click` for more complex functionality.

Step 1: Define the Command-Line Tool:

```python
python

import argparse
import os
import shutil

# Create the parser
parser = argparse.ArgumentParser(description="A
command-line tool to manage system tasks.")

# Define command-line arguments
```

```python
parser.add_argument('action',   choices=['list',
'create', 'delete'], help="Action to perform:
list, create, or delete")
parser.add_argument('path', type=str, help="The
directory or file path")
parser.add_argument('--name',           type=str,
help="The name of the directory to create",
default=None)

# Parse the arguments
args = parser.parse_args()

# Perform the action based on user input
if args.action == 'list':
    # List all files in the directory
    if os.path.isdir(args.path):
        files = os.listdir(args.path)
        print(f"Files in {args.path}:")
        for file in files:
            print(file)
    else:
        print(f"{args.path} is not a valid
directory.")

elif args.action == 'create':
    # Create a new directory
    if args.name:
        new_dir    =    os.path.join(args.path,
args.name)
```

168

```
        os.makedirs(new_dir, exist_ok=True)
        print(f"Directory '{args.name}' created
at {args.path}.")
    else:
        print("Please provide a name for the
directory using the --name option.")

elif args.action == 'delete':
    # Delete a file
    if os.path.isfile(args.path):
        os.remove(args.path)
        print(f"File {args.path} deleted.")
    else:
        print(f"{args.path} is not a valid
file.")
```

Explanation:

- The tool supports three actions: `list`, `create`, and `delete`.
    - `list`: Lists the files in the given directory.
    - `create`: Creates a new directory inside the specified path.
    - `delete`: Deletes a file at the specified path.
- `argparse` is used to parse the command-line arguments and perform the corresponding action.

Step 2: Running the Command-Line Tool

- To list the files in a directory:

```bash
python tool.py list /path/to/directory
```

- To create a new directory:

```bash
python tool.py create /path/to/directory --name new_folder
```

- To delete a file:

```bash
python tool.py delete /path/to/file.txt
```

Example Output for Listing Files:

```bash
Files in /path/to/directory:
file1.txt
file2.txt
folder1
```

Example Output for Creating a Directory:

bash

Directory   'new_folder'   created   at
/path/to/directory.

Example Output for Deleting a File:

bash

File /path/to/file.txt deleted.

In this chapter, we learned how to create **cross-platform command-line tools** using Python. These tools allow you to automate and manage various system tasks efficiently. We explored the `argparse` and `click` libraries for handling command-line arguments and options, and saw how they can be used to build flexible and user-friendly tools.

We then implemented a **real-world example** of a command-line tool that allows users to perform common system tasks, such as listing files, creating directories, and deleting files, with simple commands.

Whether you're automating system processes, building utilities, or managing files, Python's command-line tools provide a powerful way to create efficient and cross-platform applications.

Chapter 15

Packaging and Distributing Python Applications

How to Package and Distribute Your Python Applications for Different Platforms

When you develop a Python application, it's often necessary to distribute it to users who may not have Python installed. Packaging your Python application into a standalone executable allows it to run on any platform without requiring the end user to set up a Python environment. This is particularly important for deploying desktop applications, utilities, and tools that need to be accessible to users with minimal setup.

In this chapter, we'll explore how to package and distribute your Python applications across different platforms, including **Windows**, **macOS**, and **Linux**. We'll focus on tools like **PyInstaller**, **cx_Freeze**, and **py2exe** to create standalone executables.

Using PyInstaller, cx_Freeze, and py2exe to Create Standalone Executables

1. PyInstaller:

- **PyInstaller** is one of the most popular tools for converting Python programs into standalone executables. It works by bundling your Python script, the Python interpreter, and all necessary libraries into a single executable file. PyInstaller supports **Windows**, **macOS**, and **Linux**, making it a great choice for cross-platform distribution.

Basic Usage of PyInstaller:

- To install PyInstaller, use `pip`:

bash

```
pip install pyinstaller
```

- To package your Python script into an executable:

bash

```
pyinstaller --onefile your_script.py
```

- **Explanation**:

174

    ○ `--onefile`: Tells PyInstaller to bundle everything into a single executable file.

    ○ The executable will be created in the `dist/` directory.

Example (Packaging a Python script):

```
bash
```

```
pyinstaller --onefile myapp.py
```

- After running the command, PyInstaller will create a single executable file (`myapp.exe` on Windows, `myapp` on Linux/macOS) that you can distribute to users.

2. cx_Freeze:

- **cx_Freeze** is another tool that can be used to create standalone executables from Python scripts. Like PyInstaller, it bundles Python programs with their dependencies and the Python interpreter. It also supports cross-platform development for **Windows**, **macOS**, and **Linux**.

Basic Usage of cx_Freeze:

- To install cx_Freeze:

bash

pip install cx_Freeze

- To create an executable with cx_Freeze, you typically need to create a setup script (setup.py) that specifies how to build your application.

Example setup.py for cx_Freeze:

python

```
from cx_Freeze import setup, Executable

# Define the executable
exe    =    Executable(script="your_script.py",
base="Console")

# Define the setup
setup(
    name="YourAppName",
    version="1.0",
    description="Your application description",
    executables=[exe]
)
```

- To build the executable, run:

bash

```
python setup.py build
```

- This will generate a directory (build/) containing the executable, which can be distributed.

3. py2exe:

- **py2exe** is a Windows-only tool used to convert Python scripts into standalone executables for the **Windows** platform. It's suitable for distributing Python applications to users who don't have Python installed.

Basic Usage of py2exe:

- To install py2exe:

```
bash
```

```
pip install py2exe
```

- The process is similar to **cx_Freeze** and involves creating a setup script.

Example setup.py for py2exe:

```
python
```

```
from distutils.core import setup
```

177

```
import py2exe
```

```
setup(console=["your_script.py"])
```

- To build the executable, run:

```
bash
```

```
python setup.py py2exe
```

- This will create a `dist/` directory containing the executable, which can be distributed.

Real-World Example: Packaging a Python Desktop App for Windows, macOS, and Linux

Let's walk through an example where we package a simple Python desktop application using **PyInstaller** for **cross-platform distribution**. Our application will be a basic desktop app that prints a message when the user clicks a button.

Step 1: Creating the Python App (Simple GUI App)

First, let's create a simple Python app using **Tkinter**, the standard Python library for creating GUIs.

178

```
python

import tkinter as tk

# Create the main window
root = tk.Tk()
root.title("Simple App")

# Create a label
label = tk.Label(root, text="Hello, World!")
label.pack(padx=10, pady=10)

# Create a button that updates the label
def on_click():
    label.config(text="Button Clicked!")

button = tk.Button(root, text="Click Me",
command=on_click)
button.pack(padx=10, pady=10)

# Run the app
root.mainloop()
```

- This app displays a button, and when clicked, it updates the label to "Button Clicked!".

Step 2: Packaging the App with PyInstaller

179

Now, we'll package this simple GUI app into standalone executables for **Windows**, **macOS**, and **Linux** using PyInstaller.

1. Install PyInstaller if you haven't already:

```bash
pip install pyinstaller
```

2. Package the app for **Windows**:

```bash
pyinstaller --onefile --windowed app.py
```

  o `--onefile`: Creates a single executable file.
  o `--windowed`: Tells PyInstaller not to open a terminal window (for GUI applications).

After running the command, the executable will be located in the `dist/` directory. You can distribute this executable to Windows users without requiring them to install Python.

3. Package the app for **macOS**:

```bash
```

180

```
pyinstaller --onefile --windowed app.py
```

- The same command works for macOS, but make sure you have **Xcode** and the required dependencies installed for PyInstaller to build macOS executables.

4. Package the app for **Linux**:

```bash
```

```
pyinstaller --onefile --windowed app.py
```

- This command will create an executable for Linux, and you can distribute it to Linux users. Ensure that the target Linux system has the necessary libraries installed.

Step 3: Distributing the Executable

- After packaging your Python app into an executable, you can share the file with users:
  - **Windows**: Share the `.exe` file.
  - **macOS**: Share the `.app` bundle or the executable.
  - **Linux**: Share the executable, ensuring the user has execute permissions (`chmod +x app`).

If you want to distribute your app via **installer packages** (e.g., `.msi` for Windows, `.dmg` for macOS), you can use additional tools like **Inno Setup** (for Windows) or **dmgbuild** (for macOS).

In this chapter, we covered how to **package and distribute** your Python applications across different platforms using tools like **PyInstaller, cx_Freeze**, and **py2exe**. We walked through creating a simple GUI app and packaging it into standalone executables for **Windows, macOS**, and **Linux**.

Key Takeaways:

- **PyInstaller** is a powerful tool for packaging Python applications into standalone executables, supporting multiple platforms.
- **cx_Freeze** and **py2exe** are additional tools that can also be used to create standalone executables, with py2exe being Windows-specific.
- Python's versatility allows you to easily package your application for different platforms, ensuring that your

users can run your software without needing to install Python.

With the tools and techniques covered in this chapter, you can now distribute your Python applications as standalone executables, providing an easy and seamless experience for your end users.

Chapter 16

Creating Cross-Platform Desktop Applications with Python

Using Tkinter, PyQt, and Kivy for Building Cross-Platform GUIs

Creating cross-platform desktop applications is a common use case for Python, and several libraries are available to help you build **Graphical User Interfaces (GUIs)** that work seamlessly across **Windows, macOS**, and **Linux**. The three most commonly used libraries for this purpose are **Tkinter, PyQt**, and **Kivy**. Each of these frameworks has its strengths and can be used for different types of applications.

1. Tkinter:

- **Tkinter** is the standard Python library for building simple GUI applications. It is lightweight, easy to use, and comes bundled with Python, meaning you don't need to install anything extra to use it.
- **Pros**:
  - Built into Python, no additional installation required.
  - Simple and lightweight.

- **Cons**:
    - ○ Limited in terms of advanced UI features compared to more powerful frameworks like **PyQt** or **Kivy**.
- **Use Cases**: Basic applications like calculators, to-do lists, or other small utilities.

2. PyQt:

- **PyQt** is a set of Python bindings for the **Qt** application framework, which is used for creating powerful and professional-looking cross-platform applications. It offers advanced UI features, supports custom widgets, and provides access to Qt's vast ecosystem.
- **Pros**:
    - ○ Rich in features, ideal for creating sophisticated desktop applications.
    - ○ Supports custom widgets, multimedia, and advanced UI elements.
- **Cons**:
    - ○ Steeper learning curve compared to Tkinter.
- **Use Cases**: Applications requiring advanced UIs, such as media players, complex editors, or data visualization tools.

3. Kivy:

- **Kivy** is a modern, open-source Python framework that allows you to build multi-touch applications. It is particularly well-suited for building **mobile** applications in addition to desktop apps.
- **Pros**:
  - Supports touch-based interfaces and gestures.
  - Cross-platform (including mobile platforms like **Android** and **iOS**).
- **Cons**:
  - Different in design compared to traditional desktop UI frameworks, making it less intuitive for developers familiar with other GUI toolkits.
- **Use Cases**: Mobile and desktop applications, especially those requiring touch interfaces and multitouch support.

Handling Native Operating System Integrations (File Dialogs, Notifications)

When building cross-platform desktop applications, it's important to integrate with the native features of the operating system. This includes things like file dialogs for opening and saving files, notifications for alerts or reminders, and system tray icons for background tasks. Each

GUI framework provides different ways to integrate these native features.

1. File Dialogs:

- **Tkinter**: Tkinter provides a file dialog module that allows you to prompt the user to open or save files using the native file picker dialog of the operating system.
- **PyQt**: PyQt has a built-in file dialog widget that mimics the native file dialog for each operating system.
- **Kivy**: Kivy also provides a basic file chooser dialog, though it's not as feature-rich as Tkinter or PyQt's dialogs.

2. Notifications:

- **Tkinter**: Tkinter doesn't provide native notifications, but you can use libraries like `plyer` to handle notifications across platforms.
- **PyQt**: PyQt allows integration with native notification systems using the **QtWidgets.QSystemTrayIcon** class.
- **Kivy**: Like Tkinter, Kivy doesn't provide native notifications out of the box, but you can use `plyer` or integrate platform-specific notification libraries.

3. System Tray Icons:

- **PyQt**: You can create system tray applications using `QSystemTrayIcon`, allowing you to put an icon in the system tray and provide options for background tasks.
- **Tkinter**: Tkinter doesn't natively support system tray icons, but you can use third-party libraries such as `pystray` to achieve this.
- **Kivy**: Kivy doesn't natively support system tray icons either, but `pystray` can be used for this purpose.

Real-World Example: Developing a File Organizer App with a GUI Using PyQt

In this real-world example, we'll build a **File Organizer** desktop application using **PyQt**. This app will allow users to:

- Select a folder.
- View the files in that folder.
- Move or rename files from one directory to another using the GUI.

Let's break this down into steps:

Step 1: Installing PyQt5

First, you need to install PyQt5. You can do this with pip:

```bash
bash
```

```
pip install pyqt5
```

Step 2: Creating the Basic GUI

We'll create a basic PyQt application with a window that includes a file dialog for selecting folders, a list view for displaying files, and buttons for organizing files.

```python
python

import sys
import os
from PyQt5.QtWidgets import QApplication,
QWidget, QVBoxLayout, QPushButton, QFileDialog,
QListView, QStringListModel

class FileOrganizerApp(QWidget):
    def __init__(self):
        super().__init__()

        # Initialize the window
        self.setWindowTitle('File Organizer')
        self.setGeometry(100, 100, 500, 300)

        # Create a layout
```

189

```python
self.layout = QVBoxLayout()

# Create a button for selecting a folder
self.select_folder_button                =
QPushButton('Select Folder')

self.select_folder_button.clicked.connect(self.
select_folder)

self.layout.addWidget(self.select_folder_button
)

# Create a list view to display the files
self.file_list_view = QListView()

self.layout.addWidget(self.file_list_view)

# Create a button to move files
self.move_file_button                    =
QPushButton('Move Files')

self.move_file_button.clicked.connect(self.move
_files)

self.layout.addWidget(self.move_file_button)

# Set the layout
self.setLayout(self.layout)
```

```python
        # Initialize file list
        self.files = []

    def select_folder(self):
        folder_path                                =
QFileDialog.getExistingDirectory(self,   'Select
Folder')
        if folder_path:
            self.load_files(folder_path)

    def load_files(self, folder_path):
        """Load the files from the selected
folder and display them in the list view."""
        self.files    =    [f    for    f    in
os.listdir(folder_path)                        if
os.path.isfile(os.path.join(folder_path, f))]
        model = QStringListModel(self.files)
        self.file_list_view.setModel(model)

    def move_files(self):
        """Move the selected file to a new
directory."""
        selected_indexes                          =
self.file_list_view.selectedIndexes()
        if selected_indexes:
            selected_file                          =
self.files[selected_indexes[0].row()]
            current_dir = os.getcwd()
```

191

```
            source_path                    =
os.path.join(current_dir, selected_file)
            destination_dir                =
QFileDialog.getExistingDirectory(self,   'Select
Destination Folder')
            if destination_dir:
                destination_path           =
os.path.join(destination_dir, selected_file)
                os.rename(source_path,
destination_path)

self.load_files(destination_dir)
                print(f"Moved {selected_file} to
{destination_dir}")


if __name__ == '__main__':
    app = QApplication(sys.argv)
    window = FileOrganizerApp()
    window.show()
    sys.exit(app.exec_())
```

Explanation:

- The `FileOrganizerApp` class inherits from `QWidget` and contains all the GUI components.
- The **Select Folder** button uses `QFileDialog.getExistingDirectory` to prompt the user to choose a folder.

192

- The **file list** is displayed in a `QListView`, and the files in the selected folder are loaded into the list.
- The **Move Files** button allows the user to select a file from the list and move it to a new directory.

Step 3: Running the Application

Run the script:

```bash

python file_organizer.py
```

This will open a GUI window where you can select a folder, view the files, and move them to another directory.

In this chapter, we explored how to build cross-platform desktop applications using **Python** and libraries like **Tkinter**, **PyQt**, and **Kivy**. These frameworks provide the tools to create powerful graphical applications that work seamlessly across **Windows**, **macOS**, and **Linux**.

We also learned how to handle native integrations, such as file dialogs and notifications, and how to work with system-specific features in a cross-platform manner.

In the real-world example, we developed a **File Organizer** application using **PyQt** that allows users to select a folder, view files, and move them between directories using a simple graphical interface. PyQt's powerful features, such as **file dialogs** and **list views**, make it an excellent choice for building complex desktop applications.

By mastering these frameworks and techniques, you can develop robust, user-friendly cross-platform applications that take full advantage of Python's capabilities. Whether you're building a simple utility or a complex desktop app, these tools will help you create efficient and portable software.

Part 5

Specialized Cross-Platform Development

Chapter 17

Developing Cross-Platform Mobile Applications

Introduction to Mobile Development with Python Using Kivy, BeeWare, and PyQt

Mobile app development has traditionally been dominated by languages like Java, Swift, and Kotlin. However, Python provides several powerful tools and frameworks that allow developers to build **cross-platform mobile applications** that run on both **Android** and **iOS**. This allows Python developers to extend their skills into the mobile development space.

In this chapter, we will explore three major frameworks for developing mobile apps with Python: **Kivy**, **BeeWare**, and **PyQt**. We'll focus on how to set up these environments for mobile development, their key features, and a real-world example of building a mobile app using Kivy.

1. Kivy: A Framework for Multi-Touch Mobile and Desktop Applications

Kivy is an open-source Python framework that allows developers to create mobile and desktop applications with a focus on **multi-touch** and **gesture-based** UIs. It is one of the most popular frameworks for building **cross-platform mobile applications** and supports Android, iOS, Windows, macOS, and Linux.

- **Key Features**:
    - Cross-platform: Works on Android, iOS, Windows, macOS, and Linux.
    - Multi-touch support: Ideal for applications that require touch interactions.
    - Easy to learn and use: Suitable for both beginners and advanced developers.
    - Rich UI toolkit: Supports complex layouts, widgets, and animations.
- **Installation**: To get started with Kivy, you need to install it first:

```bash

pip install kivy
```

197

- **Setting up Kivy for Android/iOS**:
  - For **Android**: Kivy provides a tool called **Buildozer** that simplifies the process of building and packaging Kivy apps for Android.
    - To install Buildozer:

    bash

    ```
    pip install buildozer
    ```

    - After creating your Kivy app, you can use Buildozer to create an APK file:

    bash

    ```
    buildozer android debug
    ```

  - For **iOS**: Building Kivy apps for iOS requires a macOS machine with **Xcode** installed. Use **Kivy-ios** to package the app for iOS devices.
    - To install Kivy-iOS:

    bash

    ```
    pip install kivy-ios
    ```

2. BeeWare: Building Native Mobile Apps with Python

BeeWare is a collection of tools and libraries for building cross-platform native applications using Python. It provides the ability to create applications with native UIs that run on iOS, Android, Windows, macOS, and Linux. Unlike Kivy, which uses its own set of widgets, BeeWare allows you to use the native widgets and APIs of each platform, providing a more **native look and feel**.

- **Key Features**:
  - Native UI components: Uses platform-specific widgets for Android, iOS, and desktop platforms.
  - Pythonic API: Provides an easy-to-use API that is consistent across platforms.
  - Integration with native OS features.
- **Installation**: To get started with BeeWare, you can install the **Toga** library, which is the BeeWare framework for building mobile and desktop applications.

```bash
pip install toga
```

- **Setting up BeeWare for Android/iOS**:

199

o To set up BeeWare for mobile development, you need to install **Briefcase** (a tool to package apps).

- To install Briefcase:

```bash
pip install briefcase
```

- For **Android**: You need to set up the Android SDK and NDK. Briefcase simplifies packaging your app for Android:

```bash
briefcase new android
```

o For **iOS**: You need a macOS machine with Xcode installed. Once configured, you can package your app for iOS using Briefcase.

```bash
briefcase build iOS
```

3. PyQt for Mobile App Development

PyQt is a set of Python bindings for the Qt application framework, commonly used for building desktop applications. While **Qt** itself doesn't natively support mobile development, PyQt can be used in combination with **Qt for Android** or **Qt for iOS** to build mobile applications.

- **Key Features**:
    - Powerful GUI capabilities with extensive widget support.
    - Native look and feel for desktop applications.
    - Can be extended to mobile applications using Qt's mobile tools.
- **Limitations**:
    - Setting up PyQt for mobile development is more complex than Kivy or BeeWare, and might require deeper knowledge of Qt.

Setting up Mobile Development Environments for Android and iOS

Before diving into app development, you need to set up your development environment for building mobile apps with Python.

1. Android Development Setup:

- Install **Android Studio** to get the Android SDK and NDK.
- Install **Buildozer** for Kivy (as described earlier) to build Android apps.
- For **BeeWare**, use **Briefcase** to build Android applications.

2. iOS Development Setup:

- For **macOS**, you need **Xcode** installed to build and run iOS applications.
- Kivy and BeeWare both support iOS development through specific tools (Kivy-iOS for Kivy and Briefcase for BeeWare).
- For iOS, use **Kivy-ios** or **Briefcase** to package apps.

Real-World Example: Creating a Simple Mobile To-Do List App Using Kivy

Now, let's walk through a simple **To-Do List** app using **Kivy**, which will work on Android, iOS, and desktop platforms. The app will allow the user to add and remove tasks.

Step 1: Install Kivy

First, install Kivy if you haven't already:

bash

```
pip install kivy
```

Step 2: Creating the To-Do List App

Here's the Python code for a simple to-do list app with Kivy:

python

```
from kivy.app import App
from kivy.uix.boxlayout import BoxLayout
from kivy.uix.textinput import TextInput
from kivy.uix.button import Button
from kivy.uix.label import Label
from kivy.uix.scrollview import ScrollView

class TodoApp(App):
    def build(self):
        self.tasks = []

        # Create the layout
        layout                              =
BoxLayout(orientation='vertical')

        # Create the text input for task entry
```

203

```python
        self.task_input                        =
TextInput(hint_text="Enter    a    new    task",
size_hint_y=None, height=40)
        layout.add_widget(self.task_input)

        # Create the button to add tasks
        add_button    =    Button(text="Add    Task",
size_hint_y=None, height=40)
        add_button.bind(on_press=self.add_task)
        layout.add_widget(add_button)

        # Create the scrollable area to display
tasks
        self.scroll_view = ScrollView()
        self.task_list                        =
BoxLayout(orientation='vertical',
size_hint_y=None)

self.task_list.bind(minimum_height=self.task_li
st.setter('height'))


self.scroll_view.add_widget(self.task_list)
        layout.add_widget(self.scroll_view)

        return layout

    def add_task(self, instance):
        task_text = self.task_input.text
```

```
        if task_text:
            task_label  =  Label(text=task_text,
size_hint_y=None, height=40)

self.task_list.add_widget(task_label)
            self.tasks.append(task_text)        #
Store the task in the list
            self.task_input.text = ""   # Clear
the input field

if __name__ == "__main__":
    TodoApp().run()
```

Explanation:

- The app uses a `BoxLayout` with a vertical orientation to arrange the widgets.
- It includes a `TextInput` for entering new tasks, a `Button` to add tasks, and a `ScrollView` to display the list of tasks.
- When a task is added, it is displayed in the scrollable list, and the input field is cleared.

Step 3: Running the Application

To run the app on your desktop:

bash

```
python todo_app.py
```

Step 4: Packaging for Android (Using Buildozer)

To package the app for Android, use **Buildozer**. First, install Buildozer:

```bash
```

```
pip install buildozer
```

Then, create a Buildozer spec file:

```bash
```

```
buildozer init
```

Edit the generated `buildozer.spec` file (set the app name, package, and version), and then run:

```bash
```

```
buildozer android debug
```

This will create an APK file that you can install on your Android device.

In this chapter, we explored the tools available for **cross-platform mobile development** with Python. We covered three major frameworks:

- **Kivy**: A versatile framework for building mobile and desktop applications with Python.
- **BeeWare**: A set of tools that allow you to build native applications using Python.
- **PyQt**: While primarily used for desktop apps, PyQt can be extended to mobile platforms using **Qt for Android/iOS**.

We also learned how to **set up mobile development environments** for both **Android** and **iOS**, and we walked through the development of a **simple To-Do List app** using Kivy, which works on all platforms. By mastering these tools, you can expand your Python skills into mobile development, building apps that run across different platforms with ease.

Chapter 18

Python in Data Science and Machine Learning

Using Python Libraries like NumPy, Pandas, Scikit-learn, and TensorFlow for Cross-Platform Data Processing and Machine Learning

Python is one of the most popular languages for data science and machine learning, thanks to its rich ecosystem of libraries and frameworks. These tools provide easy-to-use, high-level abstractions for performing complex data processing, statistical analysis, and building machine learning models. The power of Python is in its ability to build cross-platform solutions, enabling data processing and machine learning models to be deployed on a wide range of platforms, from **desktops** to **servers** and even **mobile**.

In this chapter, we will explore some of the most widely used libraries in the Python ecosystem for data science and machine learning, such as **NumPy**, **Pandas**, **Scikit-learn**, and **TensorFlow**. We will also go through the process of building machine learning models that can be deployed across different platforms.

1. NumPy: Efficient Data Structures and Numerical Computing

NumPy is the foundation for scientific computing in Python. It provides support for **large, multi-dimensional arrays and matrices** as well as a collection of mathematical functions to operate on these arrays. NumPy is particularly useful for data processing and mathematical computations and forms the backbone for other data science libraries like **Pandas** and **Scikit-learn**.

- **Key Features**:
  - **Array objects**: The `ndarray` is a core data structure in NumPy, which allows efficient storage and manipulation of large datasets.
  - **Mathematical functions**: NumPy provides a wide range of functions for mathematical operations on arrays, such as **linear algebra** operations, **Fourier transforms**, and **random sampling**.
- **Common Use Cases**:
  - Data manipulation and transformation.

o Numerical computations for machine learning algorithms.

Example:

```python

import numpy as np

# Create a NumPy array
arr = np.array([1, 2, 3, 4, 5])

# Perform an operation on the array (e.g.,
element-wise addition)
arr = arr + 10
print(arr)   # Output: [11 12 13 14 15]
```

---

2. Pandas: Data Manipulation and Analysis

Pandas is a powerful library built on top of NumPy that provides high-level data structures like **DataFrames** and **Series** for handling and analyzing structured data. It is ideal for working with **tabular data** (like spreadsheets or CSV files) and supports operations like **data cleaning**, **grouping**, **filtering**, and **aggregation**.

- **Key Features**:

- o **DataFrames**: A 2-dimensional data structure for storing tabular data with rows and columns.
- o **Data I/O**: Pandas supports reading and writing data from various formats like CSV, Excel, JSON, SQL, and more.
- o **Data manipulation**: Pandas provides powerful tools for filtering, merging, reshaping, and summarizing data.

- **Common Use Cases**:
  - o Data cleaning and preprocessing.
  - o Data analysis and exploration.

Example:

```python
import pandas as pd

# Create a DataFrame from a CSV file
df = pd.read_csv("data.csv")

# Perform data manipulation (e.g., filtering rows)
filtered_df = df[df['age'] > 30]
print(filtered_df)
```

3. Scikit-learn: Machine Learning Algorithms and Tools

Scikit-learn is one of the most popular libraries for machine learning in Python. It provides simple and efficient tools for **data mining** and **data analysis**. Scikit-learn supports both supervised and unsupervised learning, including **classification, regression, clustering,** and **dimensionality reduction**.

- **Key Features**:
  - A wide range of machine learning algorithms (e.g., decision trees, random forests, support vector machines, linear regression, etc.).
  - Tools for **model evaluation** and **cross-validation**.
  - **Preprocessing** utilities like scaling, encoding, and imputation.
- **Common Use Cases**:
  - Building and evaluating machine learning models.
  - Data preprocessing and feature engineering for machine learning tasks.

Example:

```python
python
```

```python
from         sklearn.model_selection      import
train_test_split
from          sklearn.ensemble         import
RandomForestRegressor
from sklearn.metrics import mean_squared_error

# Load data (e.g., using pandas)
data = pd.read_csv("stock_data.csv")

# Prepare data
X = data[['feature1', 'feature2', 'feature3']]  #
Features
y = data['price']  # Target variable

# Split data into training and test sets
X_train,    X_test,    y_train,    y_test    =
train_test_split(X,     y,      test_size=0.2,
random_state=42)

# Train a Random Forest model
model = RandomForestRegressor()
model.fit(X_train, y_train)

# Make predictions
predictions = model.predict(X_test)

# Evaluate the model
mse = mean_squared_error(y_test, predictions)
print(f"Mean Squared Error: {mse}")
```

4. TensorFlow: Deep Learning for Cross-Platform Deployment

TensorFlow is an open-source library developed by Google for deep learning and artificial intelligence. It is widely used for building complex neural networks and performing advanced machine learning tasks. TensorFlow can run on both CPUs and GPUs, making it highly scalable for large datasets.

- **Key Features**:
    - Support for building and training neural networks for deep learning.
    - Cross-platform deployment: TensorFlow models can be deployed on desktop, mobile, web, and even IoT devices.
    - TensorFlow Lite: A lightweight version of TensorFlow optimized for mobile and embedded devices.
- **Common Use Cases**:
    - Image recognition, natural language processing, and speech recognition.
    - Time series forecasting and reinforcement learning.

214

Example (Creating a simple neural network with TensorFlow):

python

```python
import tensorflow as tf
from tensorflow.keras.models import Sequential
from tensorflow.keras.layers import Dense

# Load dataset
(X_train, y_train), (X_test, y_test) = tf.keras.datasets.mnist.load_data()

# Preprocess data (flatten and normalize)
X_train = X_train.reshape(-1, 28*28).astype('float32') / 255
X_test = X_test.reshape(-1, 28*28).astype('float32') / 255

# Build a simple neural network model
model = Sequential([
    Dense(128, activation='relu', input_shape=(28*28,)),
    Dense(10, activation='softmax')
])

# Compile the model
```

```
model.compile(optimizer='adam',
loss='sparse_categorical_crossentropy',
metrics=['accuracy'])

# Train the model
model.fit(X_train, y_train, epochs=5)

# Evaluate the model
loss, accuracy = model.evaluate(X_test, y_test)
print(f"Test Accuracy: {accuracy}")
```

How to Build Machine Learning Models That Can Be Deployed on Various Platforms

To build machine learning models that can be deployed across different platforms (such as desktops, mobile devices, and cloud-based servers), the following steps are essential:

1. Model Training and Exporting:

- Use frameworks like **Scikit-learn** or **TensorFlow** to train your machine learning models. Once trained, you can export the model into a portable format.
- **Scikit-learn** models can be saved using **Pickle**:

```
python
```

216

```
import pickle
with open("model.pkl", "wb") as f:
    pickle.dump(model, f)
```

- **TensorFlow** models can be saved as `.h5` or **TensorFlow SavedModel** format:

```python
model.save("model.h5")  # Save in Keras H5 format
```

2. Model Deployment:

- For desktop and web applications, you can use **TensorFlow.js**, **TensorFlow Lite**, or **ONNX** for cross-platform deployment.
- For mobile apps, use **TensorFlow Lite** to convert models to a lightweight format suitable for iOS and Android devices.

3. Serving Models in Production:

- Once models are deployed, they can be accessed via **APIs** or integrated directly into applications.
- You can use **Flask** or **FastAPI** to serve models on a web server.

Real World Example: Developing a Simple Predictive Model for Stock Prices

Let's build a **simple predictive model** that forecasts **stock prices** using machine learning. We will use **Scikit-learn** to develop a regression model and evaluate its performance.

Step 1: Collect Data

- Obtain historical stock price data (can be done through APIs like Yahoo Finance, Alpha Vantage, or Quandl).

Step 2: Preprocess Data

- Prepare the data for training by selecting relevant features (e.g., previous stock prices, volume, and other financial indicators).

Step 3: Train the Model

- Use a regression model, such as **Linear Regression** or **Random Forest**, to predict the stock price based on the selected features.

Step 4: Evaluate and Tune the Model

- Evaluate the model's performance using metrics like **Mean Squared Error (MSE)** and **R-Squared**.

In this chapter, we explored the powerful **Python libraries** for **data science** and **machine learning**: **NumPy**, **Pandas**, **Scikit-learn**, and **TensorFlow**. We discussed how to preprocess data, build models, and evaluate their performance, all while ensuring the models are cross-platform and ready for deployment.

We also covered the **deployment process** for machine learning models, from saving the model to serving it on various platforms, whether on desktops, mobile devices, or the cloud.

Finally, through the **real-world example** of developing a predictive model for stock prices, we saw how Python's data science and machine learning ecosystem can be applied to real business problems, providing valuable insights and automation in data-driven decision-making.

Chapter 19

Building Cross-Platform Games with Python

Using Game Engines like Pygame and Godot for Python Game Development

Python is an excellent language for developing games, thanks to its simplicity and the variety of game development frameworks available. Python provides robust libraries and engines like **Pygame** and **Godot** that allow developers to create games for multiple platforms such as **Windows, macOS, Linux**, and even **mobile devices**.

In this chapter, we will discuss two widely used frameworks for Python game development: **Pygame** and **Godot**. We will cover how to write **cross-platform game code** and handle critical game development components such as **graphics, audio**, and **input devices**. Lastly, we will walk through the development of a **simple 2D game** using **Pygame**.

1. Pygame: A Simple and Popular Framework for 2D Game Development

Pygame is one of the most popular Python libraries for developing 2D games. It provides modules to handle graphics, sound, and user input, making it a great tool for beginners and hobbyists who want to quickly get into game development.

- **Key Features**:
  - **Graphics**: Pygame allows you to draw images, shapes, and text onto the game window.
  - **Audio**: It supports loading and playing sound effects and music.
  - **User Input**: Pygame can capture keyboard, mouse, and joystick input.
  - **Cross-Platform**: Pygame works on **Windows**, **macOS**, and **Linux**, making it ideal for cross-platform game development.
- **Installation**: To install Pygame, simply run:

```bash
pip install pygame
```

Example: Here's a simple example of creating a game window and displaying an image using Pygame.

```python
import pygame

# Initialize Pygame
pygame.init()

# Set up the game window
width, height = 800, 600
screen = pygame.display.set_mode((width, height))
pygame.display.set_caption('Pygame Example')

# Load an image
player_image = pygame.image.load('player.png')
player_rect = player_image.get_rect()
player_rect.center = (width // 2, height // 2)

# Game loop
running = True
while running:
    for event in pygame.event.get():
        if event.type == pygame.QUIT:
            running = False

    # Fill the screen with a color
```

222

```
screen.fill((0, 0, 0))

# Draw the player image
screen.blit(player_image, player_rect)

# Update the display
pygame.display.flip()

# Quit Pygame
pygame.quit()
```

Explanation:

- This script initializes a Pygame window and displays an image of the player character at the center of the screen. The game window updates continuously until the user closes it.

2. Godot: A More Advanced Game Engine with Python Support

Godot is a popular open-source game engine that offers support for both 2D and 3D game development. It has its own scripting language, **GDScript**, but also supports Python through the **Godot Python** plugin. Godot provides a rich set of features for creating professional-quality games and allows you to export to a wide range of platforms, including **desktop** and **mobile**.

- **Key Features**:
  - ○ **2D and 3D Game Development**: Godot allows you to develop both 2D and 3D games.
  - ○ **Cross-Platform**: It supports exporting games to **Windows, macOS, Linux, Android, iOS**, and many other platforms.
  - ○ **Visual Editor**: Godot includes a powerful visual editor for designing levels, assets, and game logic.
  - ○ **Python Support**: By using the Godot Python plugin, you can write your game logic in Python.
- **Installation**: To use Godot with Python, you first need to download the **Godot engine** from Godot's official website and install the **Godot Python plugin**.
- **Developing Cross-Platform Games**: When developing games in Godot with Python, you can write your game scripts using Python, while Godot handles the cross-platform deployment. You can export your game to different platforms using Godot's built-in export templates.

Writing Cross-Platform Game Code and Handling Graphics, Audio, and Input Devices

To build a game that works seamlessly across different platforms, it's important to use game engines and libraries that abstract away platform-specific details. Both **Pygame** and **Godot** are designed to handle these complexities for you, allowing you to focus on the game's logic and mechanics.

Here's how you handle essential game components across platforms:

1. Graphics:

- **Pygame**: Use `pygame.Surface` objects for drawing images and shapes on the screen. You can load images with `pygame.image.load()` and draw them with `screen.blit()`.
- **Godot**: Use **Sprites** for 2D graphics and **MeshInstances** for 3D models. Godot's visual editor allows you to drag and drop assets, which simplifies the workflow.

2. Audio:

- **Pygame**: Use `pygame.mixer` to load and play music and sound effects. It supports various audio formats like WAV and MP3.
- **Godot**: Godot uses its own audio system to handle background music and sound effects. You can use **AudioStreamPlayer** nodes to play sounds.

3. Input Devices:

- **Pygame**: Use `pygame.event.get()` to capture keyboard and mouse events. You can also handle gamepad inputs using `pygame.joystick`.
- **Godot**: Godot's input system allows you to capture input from the keyboard, mouse, and even touchscreen devices. It provides methods like `Input.is_key_pressed()` to check key states.

Real-World Example: Developing a Basic 2D Game Using Pygame

Let's develop a simple **2D game** using **Pygame** where the player controls a character that can move around the screen. This game will include basic features like **player movement, collision detection**, and **gameover logic**.

Step 1: Set Up the Game Window and Player Object

```python
python

import pygame
import random

# Initialize Pygame
pygame.init()

# Set up the game window
width, height = 800, 600
screen      =     pygame.display.set_mode((width,
height))
pygame.display.set_caption('Basic 2D Game')

# Colors
WHITE = (255, 255, 255)
RED = (255, 0, 0)

# Player setup
player_image = pygame.image.load('player.png')
player_rect = player_image.get_rect()
player_rect.center = (width // 2, height - 50)
player_speed = 5

# Game loop
running = True
while running:
    screen.fill(WHITE)  # Fill the screen with a
white color
```

```
# Event handling
for event in pygame.event.get():
    if event.type == pygame.QUIT:
        running = False

# Player movement
keys = pygame.key.get_pressed()
if keys[pygame.K_LEFT] and player_rect.left
> 0:
        player_rect.x -= player_speed
    if          keys[pygame.K_RIGHT]          and
player_rect.right < width:
        player_rect.x += player_speed

# Draw the player
screen.blit(player_image, player_rect)

# Update the screen
pygame.display.flip()

# Quit Pygame
pygame.quit()
```

Explanation:

- This basic Pygame application sets up a window with a player object that can move left and right using the arrow

228

keys. The game will continue to run until the user closes the window.

Step 2: Add Obstacles and Collision Detection

To make the game more interesting, let's add some obstacles that the player must avoid.

python

```python
# Obstacle setup
obstacle_width, obstacle_height = 50, 50
obstacle_speed = 5
obstacles = []

def create_obstacle():
    obstacle_x = random.randint(0, width - obstacle_width)
    obstacle_y = -obstacle_height
    obstacles.append(pygame.Rect(obstacle_x, obstacle_y, obstacle_width, obstacle_height))

# Game loop (continuation)
while running:
    screen.fill(WHITE)

    # Event handling
    for event in pygame.event.get():
        if event.type == pygame.QUIT:
```

```
        running = False

    # Create obstacles
    if random.random() < 0.02:
        create_obstacle()


    # Move and draw obstacles
    for obstacle in obstacles[:]:
        obstacle.y += obstacle_speed
        if obstacle.colliderect(player_rect):
            print("Game Over!")
            running = False  # End the game if
the player collides with an obstacle
        if obstacle.top > height:
            obstacles.remove(obstacle)
        pygame.draw.rect(screen, RED, obstacle)


    # Player movement
    keys = pygame.key.get_pressed()
    if keys[pygame.K_LEFT] and player_rect.left
> 0:
        player_rect.x -= player_speed
    if          keys[pygame.K_RIGHT]           and
player_rect.right < width:
        player_rect.x += player_speed


    # Draw the player
    screen.blit(player_image, player_rect)
```

```
    # Update the screen
    pygame.display.flip()

# Quit Pygame
pygame.quit()
```

Explanation:

- We added obstacles that fall from the top of the screen. The player must avoid these obstacles to prevent a gameover. If a collision is detected, the game ends.

In this chapter, we covered how to create **cross-platform 2D games** using Python. We discussed two popular game development frameworks, **Pygame** and **Godot**, and their key features. We also explored how to handle critical game components like **graphics**, **audio**, and **user input**.

Through the **real-world example**, we built a simple 2D game using **Pygame**, where the player controls a character and must avoid falling obstacles. The game involved basic concepts like **player movement**, **collision detection**, and **game-over logic**.

By using these frameworks, Python developers can create engaging games that run on various platforms, from desktops to mobile devices. Whether you are a beginner or an experienced developer, Python's rich ecosystem provides the tools you need to bring your game ideas to life.

Part 6

Best Practices and
Performance Optimization

Chapter 20

Writing Efficient Python Code

Performance Optimization Techniques: Profiling, Reducing Overhead, and Memory Management

In this chapter, we will focus on how to write **efficient Python code** that performs well across multiple platforms. Python, while highly readable and versatile, can sometimes suffer from performance bottlenecks due to its interpreted nature and dynamic typing. However, there are several strategies that can help optimize your Python code, making it faster and more memory-efficient.

We will cover key performance optimization techniques, including **profiling**, **reducing overhead**, and **memory management**, and how to write code that scales well with large datasets. This is crucial for applications that deal with significant amounts of data or need to run efficiently across different environments.

Profiling allows you to measure the performance of your code, helping you identify which parts are consuming the most resources, such as CPU time or memory. In Python, profiling can be done using tools like **cProfile** and **timeit**.

- **cProfile**: This is a built-in Python module that provides detailed statistics about the time spent in each function in your code. It's ideal for performance analysis.

  Example:

```python
python

import cProfile

def slow_function():
    result = 0
    for i in range(100000):
        result += i
    return result

cProfile.run('slow_function()')
```

  Explanation:

- o This will profile the `slow_function()` and print a summary of how much time was spent in each function call. This helps you pinpoint areas of the code that could be optimized.
- **timeit**: This module is useful for timing small snippets of Python code, providing accurate execution time measurements.

Example:

```python

import timeit

# Measure time taken by a loop
time_taken = timeit.timeit('for i in range(100): x = i * i', number=10000)
print(f"Time taken: {time_taken} seconds")
```

Explanation:

- o This code measures how long it takes to run a loop 10,000 times, helping you identify inefficient code blocks.

2. Reducing Overhead: Minimize Unnecessary Computations

In Python, certain operations can incur significant overhead, especially in tight loops or recursive functions. Here are some common strategies to reduce unnecessary computations:

- **Avoid Repeated Function Calls**: If you're repeatedly calling a function with the same arguments, consider caching the result or moving the computation outside the loop.

  Example:

  ```python
  python

  # Avoid recalculating the same result
  inside a loop
  result = {}
  for x in range(1000):
      if x not in result:
          result[x]                        =
  some_expensive_calculation(x)
  ```

  Explanation:

  - By caching the result, you avoid recalculating the same value multiple times, reducing overhead.

237

- **Use Built-in Functions**: Python's built-in functions are often optimized in C, so they tend to be faster than equivalent Python code written manually.

Example:

```python

# Use built-in sum instead of a loop for
summing values
numbers = range(100000)
total = sum(numbers)    # Faster than
manually summing with a loop
```

Explanation:

- o `sum()` is highly optimized and can perform better than writing a custom loop to sum the values.

- **Avoid Using Global Variables**: Accessing global variables is slower than using local ones. Always try to limit the use of global variables in performance-critical code.

3. Memory Management: Reducing Memory Usage

Efficient memory management is critical when dealing with large datasets. Python provides tools and strategies to reduce memory consumption and optimize the use of system resources.

- **Use Generators**: Instead of loading entire datasets into memory at once, you can use generators to process data on-the-fly. Generators allow you to iterate over large datasets without storing the entire dataset in memory.

  Example:

  python

  ```python
  # Using a generator to read a large file
  line by line
  def read_large_file(file_name):
      with open(file_name, 'r') as file:
          for line in file:
              yield line


  for line in read_large_file('large_file.txt'):
      process(line)    # Process each line
  without loading the entire file into memory
  ```

239

Explanation:

- o The `yield` keyword in Python allows you to return a generator, which generates data one item at a time, saving memory.

- **Use Efficient Data Structures**: When working with large datasets, selecting the right data structure is crucial. For example, **NumPy arrays** are more memory-efficient than Python lists when handling large numerical data.

Example:

```python

import numpy as np

# Use NumPy arrays instead of lists for
large numerical datasets
large_array = np.array([1, 2, 3, 4, 5])
```

Explanation:

- o NumPy arrays are more efficient in terms of both memory and performance than regular Python lists for numerical data.

- **Del and gc**: Use the `del` statement to explicitly delete variables that are no longer needed, and the `gc` module to manually trigger garbage collection.

Example:

```python
import gc

# Delete large objects explicitly when no
longer needed
del large_object

# Manually trigger garbage collection
gc.collect()
```

Explanation:

- Explicitly deleting large objects helps free up memory, and manually triggering garbage collection ensures that unused memory is reclaimed more efficiently.

Writing Efficient Python Code that Scales Across Platforms

When writing Python code that needs to scale across different platforms (e.g., from a small desktop application to a large server or mobile device), there are additional considerations:

- **Cross-Platform Libraries**: Make sure that your code uses cross-platform libraries like **NumPy**, **Pandas**, and **Scikit-learn** (for data science) or **PyInstaller** (for packaging). This ensures that your code will run seamlessly on **Windows**, **macOS**, **Linux**, and even mobile devices (using tools like **Kivy**).
- **Threading and Multiprocessing**: If your application is CPU-bound, you can improve performance by using **multiprocessing** or **threading** to distribute workloads across multiple CPU cores.

Example:

```python
python

from multiprocessing import Pool

def process_data(chunk):
    # Process a chunk of data
```

242

```
    return result

# Split data into chunks for parallel
processing
data_chunks = [data[i:i+100] for i in
range(0, len(data), 100)]
with Pool() as pool:
    results = pool.map(process_data,
data_chunks)
```

Explanation:

- By splitting the data into chunks and processing them in parallel, we can leverage multiple CPU cores, speeding up data processing.

Real-World Example: Optimizing a Python Application for Large Datasets

Let's apply these optimization techniques to a **real-world scenario** where we need to optimize a Python application that processes a large dataset, such as reading a huge CSV file, performing some transformations, and saving the results.

Step 1: Reading and Processing Data Efficiently

Instead of loading the entire dataset into memory, we use **generators** to read the file in chunks:

python

```python
import pandas as pd

def read_large_csv(file_name):
    for chunk in pd.read_csv(file_name,
chunksize=10000):
        yield chunk

# Process the file in chunks
for chunk in read_large_csv('large_data.csv'):
    process(chunk)  # Perform data processing on
each chunk
```

Step 2: Using NumPy for Efficient Data Storage

If the dataset consists of numerical values, we replace **Pandas DataFrames** with **NumPy arrays** to optimize memory usage:

python

```python
import numpy as np

# Assuming 'data' is a large list of numbers
```

244

```
data = np.array(data)    # Convert the data to a
NumPy array
```

Step 3: Using Multiprocessing for Parallel Processing

If the data processing step is computationally expensive, we can distribute the work across multiple CPU cores:

```python
from multiprocessing import Pool

def process_data(chunk):
    # Apply processing logic here
    return chunk

# Split the data into chunks for parallel
processing
chunks = np.array_split(data, 4)   # Split data
into 4 chunks
with Pool() as pool:
    processed_data   =   pool.map(process_data,
chunks)
```

Step 4: Saving the Results Efficiently

After processing, save the results in a memory-efficient format such as **HDF5** (for numerical data):

```python
import h5py

# Save the processed data in HDF5 format
with h5py.File('processed_data.h5', 'w') as f:
    f.create_dataset('dataset',
data=processed_data)
```

In this chapter, we explored several techniques to optimize Python code for **performance** and **memory usage**. We covered:

- **Profiling**: Using tools like **cProfile** and **timeit** to identify bottlenecks.
- **Reducing Overhead**: Minimizing redundant calculations and using efficient data structures.
- **Memory Management**: Using **generators** and **NumPy** to handle large datasets efficiently.

We also discussed how to write Python code that scales well across different platforms, and how to optimize an application for handling large datasets. By applying these best practices, you can significantly improve the performance and efficiency of your Python applications, whether they're running on desktops, servers, or mobile devices.

Chapter 21

Managing Dependencies and Virtual Environments

How to Manage Cross-Platform Dependencies Using `virtualenv` *and* `pipenv`

When working on a Python project, it's essential to manage **dependencies** properly to ensure your application runs smoothly across different platforms. This is especially true when deploying to multiple environments or collaborating with other developers. **Virtual environments** allow you to isolate dependencies for each project, ensuring that libraries and their versions don't conflict with those of other projects.

In this chapter, we will explore how to manage **cross-platform dependencies** using tools like `virtualenv`, `pipenv`, and `conda`. These tools will help you manage dependencies efficiently and avoid issues with package conflicts.

1. Using `virtualenv` *to Create Virtual Environments*

virtualenv is a widely-used tool for creating isolated Python environments. This allows you to install project-specific dependencies without affecting the global Python environment. `virtualenv` is particularly useful for managing dependencies across different platforms, ensuring that your project runs with the right versions of libraries, no matter the operating system.

- **Key Features**:
    - ○ Isolates dependencies for each project.
    - ○ Ensures that each project has the necessary libraries without interference from other projects.
    - ○ Works on all platforms: **Windows**, **macOS**, and **Linux**.

Installation: To install `virtualenv`, you can use `pip`:

bash

```
pip install virtualenv
```

Creating a Virtual Environment:

1. Create a new directory for your project (if it doesn't exist already):

bash

```
mkdir myproject
cd myproject
```

2. Create a virtual environment:

bash

```
virtualenv venv
```

3. Activate the virtual environment:
   o **Windows**:

   bash

   ```
   .\venv\Scripts\activate
   ```

   o **macOS/Linux**:

   bash

   ```
   source venv/bin/activate
   ```

4. You'll see the virtual environment name (e.g., `(venv)`) appear in your terminal, indicating that the

environment is active. Now, you can install dependencies using `pip`, and they will be isolated to this environment.

Deactivating the Virtual Environment: Once you are done, you can deactivate the virtual environment with:

bash

```
deactivate
```

Installing Dependencies: To install dependencies in your virtual environment, you can use `pip`:

bash

```
pip install <package_name>
```

To save the list of installed packages and their versions, you can use:

bash

```
pip freeze > requirements.txt
```

2. Using `pipenv` *for Managing Dependencies and Virtual Environments*

`pipenv` is a higher-level tool for managing both virtual environments and dependencies. It combines `pip` and `virtualenv` into one command-line tool, simplifying the management of Python projects and dependencies.

- **Key Features**:
  - Automatically creates and manages a virtual environment.
  - Uses **Pipfile** and **Pipfile.lock** to manage and lock dependencies.
  - Handles both package installation and dependency resolution.

Installation: To install `pipenv`, you can use `pip`:

bash

```
pip install pipenv
```

Creating a Virtual Environment with `pipenv`:

1. Create a new directory for your project (if it doesn't exist already):

```
bash
```

```
mkdir myproject
cd myproject
```

2. Install dependencies with `pipenv`:

```
bash
```

```
pipenv install <package_name>
```

This will create a **Pipfile** to track the installed dependencies and a **Pipfile.lock** to lock the exact versions of the dependencies.

Activating the Virtual Environment: You can activate the virtual environment created by `pipenv` with:

```
bash
```

```
pipenv shell
```

Installing Development Dependencies: For development dependencies (e.g., linters, testing frameworks), you can use the `--dev` flag:

```
bash
```

```
pipenv install <package_name> --dev
```

Locking Dependencies: To lock the dependencies and ensure that everyone working on the project is using the same versions, you can run:

bash

pipenv lock

Deactivating the Virtual Environment: To deactivate the virtual environment, simply exit the shell:

bash

exit

---

3. Dependency Management with conda

conda is an open-source package and environment management tool, commonly used in the **data science** and **machine learning** ecosystem. It can manage not only Python packages but also other languages like R, Ruby, and Java. conda is especially useful when working with packages that have complex dependencies, such as libraries that require non-Python libraries (e.g., **NumPy**, **TensorFlow**, etc.).

- **Key Features**:

254

- o Manages environments and dependencies for multiple languages.
- o Handles complex package dependencies, including those that require native libraries.
- o Works across platforms: **Windows**, **macOS**, and **Linux**.

Installation: To install `conda`, you typically install **Anaconda** or **Miniconda**, which come with `conda` preinstalled:

- Download **Anaconda** from here.
- Download **Miniconda** (a minimal version) from here.

Creating a New Conda Environment:

1. Create a new environment:

```bash

conda create --name myenv
```

2. Activate the environment:

```bash

conda activate myenv
```

3. Install packages:

```bash
conda install <package_name>
```

Deactivating the Environment: To deactivate the current conda environment:

```bash
conda deactivate
```

Exporting and Importing Environments: To share environments with others, you can export the environment configuration to a YAML file:

```bash
conda env export > environment.yml
```

To create a new environment from the YAML file:

```bash
conda env create -f environment.yml
```

Real-World Example: Setting Up and Managing Dependencies for a Python Project

Let's walk through a real-world example of setting up and managing dependencies for a Python project using `pipenv`.

Step 1: Initialize a New Python Project

1. Create a directory for your project:

```bash
mkdir myproject
cd myproject
```

2. Initialize a new **pipenv** environment:

```bash
pipenv install
```

This will automatically create a **Pipfile** in the project directory.

Step 2: Install Project Dependencies

Let's say you want to install **Flask** (for web development) and **requests** (for making HTTP requests). You can do this with the following command:

```bash
bash
```

```bash
pipenv install flask requests
```

- This will create a **Pipfile** if it doesn't already exist and add **Flask** and **requests** as dependencies.

Step 3: Install Development Dependencies

If you need a testing framework like **pytest**, you can install it as a development dependency:

```bash
bash
```

```bash
pipenv install pytest --dev
```

This will add **pytest** to the `Pipfile` under `[dev-packages]` and lock the version in the `Pipfile.lock`.

Step 4: Lock Dependencies

To lock the versions of all installed packages and ensure reproducibility across environments, run:

```
bash
```

```
pipenv lock
```

This generates the **Pipfile.lock** with the exact versions of all installed packages, ensuring that the same versions are used in all environments.

Step 5: Activate the Virtual Environment

To work within the isolated environment, activate it by running:

```
bash
```

```
pipenv shell
```

Step 6: Running the Project

Now you can start developing your project, knowing that all the dependencies are properly isolated in the virtual environment. When you're done, simply deactivate the environment with:

```
bash
```

```
exit
```

In this chapter, we learned how to manage **dependencies** and **virtual environments** effectively using tools like `virtualenv`, `pipenv`, and `conda`. These tools allow you to manage project-specific dependencies, ensuring that your Python applications run smoothly and consistently across different platforms.

Key takeaways:

- `virtualenv`: Useful for creating isolated environments where you can install dependencies for a specific project.
- `pipenv`: A more advanced tool that combines dependency management and virtual environments, making it easier to track and manage dependencies with a `Pipfile` and `Pipfile.lock`.
- `conda`: A cross-platform tool that is particularly beneficial when working with scientific packages that have complex dependencies.

We also went through a real-world example of setting up and managing dependencies for a Python project using `pipenv`, including installing both regular and development dependencies, locking versions, and managing the virtual environment. By following these best practices, you can ensure that your Python projects are reproducible, scalable, and easy to maintain.

Chapter 22

Cross-Platform Testing and Debugging

How to Test and Debug Python Applications Across Different Platforms

Testing and debugging are crucial aspects of software development, especially when working with **cross-platform** applications. Ensuring that your Python code works consistently across **Windows, macOS, Linux**, and even **mobile platforms** requires systematic testing and debugging strategies.

This chapter will focus on how to test and debug Python applications on different platforms, covering the use of tools like **unittest, pytest**, and **tox** for **cross-platform testing**. We will also demonstrate a **real-world example** of writing unit tests for a Python web app and running those tests on multiple platforms.

1. Testing Python Applications Across Platforms

When writing cross-platform Python applications, it is important to ensure that your code behaves the same way on all platforms. This involves setting up testing frameworks that can run on multiple operating systems and automating the process to catch any platform-specific bugs or issues.

- **Key Challenges**:
    - Platform-specific bugs (e.g., file path differences, OS-specific libraries).
    - Ensuring dependencies are correctly installed on different platforms.
    - Automating tests across platforms to save time and effort.

2. Using unittest for Cross-Platform Testing

The **unittest** module is the built-in Python testing framework. It is based on the xUnit framework, which is a popular framework for writing and running unit tests. unittest is platform-agnostic, meaning it can be used to write tests that run on **any platform** without modification.

- **Key Features**:

263

o **Test cases**: Grouping tests into logical units.

o **Assertions**: Verifying if the results are correct.

o **Test suites**: Running multiple tests together.

Example: Basic unittest Usage

python

```python
import unittest

def add(a, b):
    return a + b

class TestMathFunctions(unittest.TestCase):
    def test_add(self):
        self.assertEqual(add(1, 2), 3)
        self.assertEqual(add(-1, 1), 0)
        self.assertEqual(add(0, 0), 0)

if __name__ == '__main__':
    unittest.main()
```

Explanation:

- This code defines a simple add() function and a test class TestMathFunctions with a test method test_add(). The assertEqual assertions check

264

whether the `add()` function produces the correct results.

- Running the `unittest.main()` will run all tests in the file.

---

3. Using `pytest` for Cross-Platform Testing

`pytest` is a more flexible and powerful testing framework compared to `unittest`. It supports **fixtures**, **parameterized testing**, and rich output for debugging. `pytest` can also run on all platforms and integrates seamlessly with other tools for cross-platform testing.

- **Key Features**:
  - **Fixtures**: Set up and tear down test data.
  - **Parameterization**: Easily test a function with multiple inputs.
  - **Rich output**: Helps debug with detailed error messages.

Example: Basic `pytest` Usage

```python

import pytest
```

```python
def multiply(a, b):
    return a * b

@pytest.mark.parametrize("a, b, result", [
    (1, 2, 2),
    (2, 3, 6),
    (-1, 1, -1),
    (0, 5, 0)
])
def test_multiply(a, b, result):
    assert multiply(a, b) == result
```

Explanation:

- The `@pytest.mark.parametrize` decorator allows us to run the `test_multiply()` function with different sets of inputs (a, b, and `result`), making the test more comprehensive.

- `pytest` provides detailed output, making it easier to spot failing tests.

---

4. Using tox for Cross-Platform Testing Automation

tox is a tool used for automating testing in multiple Python environments. It is particularly useful for running tests across different versions of Python or on different operating systems. With tox, you can create a configuration file (tox.ini) that specifies the environments and dependencies for each test run.

- **Key Features**:
  - **Cross-platform support**: Run tests on multiple Python versions and environments.
  - **Automation**: Automatically manage environments and dependencies.
  - **Integration with pytest**: Works well with pytest for cross-platform testing.

Setting up tox for Cross-Platform Testing

1. **Install tox**:

```bash
pip install tox
```

2. **Create a tox.ini configuration file**:

```ini
[tox]
envlist = py38, py39

[testenv]
deps = pytest
```

267

```
commands = pytest
```

Explanation:

- The `envlist` specifies the Python versions (e.g., `py38`, `py39`) to test against.
- The `[testenv]` section installs `pytest` and runs it in the specified environments.

3. **Run tox:**

```bash
bash
```

```
tox
```

Explanation:

- `tox` will automatically create virtual environments for Python 3.8 and Python 3.9, install the dependencies, and run the tests.

---

5. Real-World Example: Writing Unit Tests for a Python Web App and Running Them on Different Platforms

Let's consider a **Python web app** built with **Flask**. We will write unit tests for this app using **pytest** and run them on multiple platforms with **tox**.

268

Step 1: Create the Flask Web App

python

```python
from flask import Flask

app = Flask(__name__)

@app.route('/')
def hello_world():
    return 'Hello, World!'

if __name__ == '__main__':
    app.run()
```

Step 2: Write Unit Tests Using `pytest`

python

```python
import pytest
from app import app

@pytest.fixture
def client():
    with app.test_client() as client:
        yield client

def test_hello(client):
    response = client.get('/')
    assert response.data == b'Hello, World!'
```
269

```
assert response.status_code == 200
```

Explanation:

- The `test_hello()` function sends a **GET request** to the root route (/) of the Flask app and asserts that the response contains the correct data and status code.

Step 3: Set Up tox for Cross-Platform Testing

1. Install `tox` and dependencies:

   ```bash
   bash
   ```

   ```bash
   pip install tox pytest Flask
   ```

2. Create the `tox.ini` configuration file:

   ```ini
   ini
   ```

   ```ini
   [tox]
   envlist = py38, py39, py310

   [testenv]
   deps = pytest
   commands = pytest
   ```

3. Run the tests with `tox`:

```
bash
```

```
tox
```

Explanation:

- `tox` will create virtual environments for Python 3.8, 3.9, and 3.10, install the dependencies, and run the unit tests for the Flask app on all of these environments.

---

6. Debugging Python Applications Across Platforms

In addition to testing, debugging is an essential part of cross-platform development. Some key debugging techniques include:

- **Using Logging**: Python's built-in `logging` module allows you to output messages that can help trace bugs.
    - o Example:

      ```python
      python
      ```

      ```python
      import logging
      logging.basicConfig(level=logging.D
      EBUG)
      ```

271

```
logging.debug('This    is    a    debug
message')
```

- **Platform-Specific Debugging Tools**:
  - ○ **Windows**: You can use **Visual Studio Code** or **PyCharm** for debugging on Windows.
  - ○ **macOS/Linux**: Tools like **pdb** (Python's debugger) can be used directly in the terminal.
- **Remote Debugging**: If you're running your app on a different platform (e.g., remote server or mobile device), you can use **remote debugging** tools in IDEs like **PyCharm** or **VS Code**.

In this chapter, we explored how to effectively **test** and **debug** Python applications across different platforms. We learned how to use popular testing frameworks like `unittest`, `pytest`, and `tox` to write cross-platform tests, ensuring that our applications perform as expected on various operating systems.

We also walked through a **real-world example** of writing unit tests for a Flask web application and running them on multiple platforms using **tox**. Additionally, we covered

272

debugging strategies that can help you troubleshoot issues effectively across platforms, ensuring that your Python applications are robust, efficient, and reliable.

By following the best practices and utilizing these tools, you can ensure that your Python applications are thoroughly tested, debugged, and optimized for cross-platform performance.

Part 7

The Future of Python and Cross-Platform Development

Chapter 23

The Role of Python in Modern Software Development

Python's Evolving Role in Web Development, AI, IoT, and More

Python has firmly established itself as one of the most versatile programming languages, powering everything from **web applications** to **artificial intelligence** (AI) and **Internet of Things** (IoT) devices. Its ease of use, vast ecosystem of libraries, and cross-platform capabilities make Python an ideal choice for modern software development across a wide range of domains.

In this chapter, we will explore Python's evolving role in several key areas of modern software development, including **web development**, **AI**, **IoT**, and its adoption in cutting-edge development paradigms like **microservices** and **serverless architectures**.

1. Python in Web Development

Python has been a dominant force in **web development** for years, particularly in the backend. With frameworks like **Django** and **Flask**, Python has become the go-to language for building **robust web applications** quickly and efficiently.

- **Django**: A high-level Python framework that encourages rapid development and clean, pragmatic design. It provides a **batteries-included** approach, offering pre-configured components like authentication, ORM (Object-Relational Mapping), and URL routing.
- **Flask**: A micro-framework that gives developers more control over their application architecture. It's lightweight and flexible, making it a great choice for small applications or when you need more customization.
- **FastAPI**: A modern, high-performance framework for building APIs with Python. It's gaining popularity for creating **RESTful APIs** and is optimized for **speed** and **data validation**.

Python's integration with web development technologies continues to grow. In recent years, **WebAssembly** support and **GraphQL** integrations have also emerged as areas where Python is being increasingly used.

Key Libraries/Technologies:

- **Django** and **Flask** for backend development.
- **FastAPI** for modern APIs.
- **Jinja2** for templating.
- **Celery** for handling asynchronous tasks.

---

2. Python in Artificial Intelligence (AI) and Machine Learning (ML)

Python's dominance in **artificial intelligence** and **machine learning** is unparalleled. Libraries like **TensorFlow**, **PyTorch**, **Keras**, and **Scikit-learn** provide everything from building simple models to complex deep learning networks.

- **TensorFlow**: An open-source platform developed by Google for machine learning. It provides tools for developing and deploying machine learning models in a wide variety of environments.
- **PyTorch**: A deep learning framework developed by Facebook, widely used for research and production-level

277

applications. It is known for its dynamic computation graph and ease of use.

- **Scikit-learn**: A simple and powerful tool for data mining and machine learning, making it accessible for those new to the field.
- **Keras**: A user-friendly API for building neural networks that works on top of TensorFlow.

Python's role in **AI** and **ML** will only continue to expand as the field grows. From **data preprocessing** to **deep learning**, Python provides a rich ecosystem for developing AI models, making it the language of choice for AI developers.

Key Libraries/Technologies:

- **TensorFlow** and **PyTorch** for deep learning.
- **Scikit-learn** for machine learning algorithms.
- **NumPy** and **Pandas** for data manipulation and analysis.
- **Jupyter Notebooks** for interactive development.

---

3. Python in Internet of Things (IoT)

Python's simple syntax, along with its support for multiple platforms, has made it a popular choice for developing **IoT applications**. Python is used in **microcontrollers** (like the

Raspberry Pi), **sensors**, and **actuators**, allowing developers to create prototypes and production systems in the IoT space quickly.

- **Raspberry Pi**: Python is the primary language for programming the **Raspberry Pi**, a low-cost microcomputer used in many IoT projects. The ability to write Python code for controlling sensors, processing data, and communicating with the cloud has made it the platform of choice for IoT developers.

- **MicroPython**: A lightweight version of Python that runs on microcontrollers, enabling developers to build embedded IoT applications efficiently.

- **MQTT and CoAP**: These lightweight communication protocols are widely used in IoT, and Python libraries like **Paho MQTT** and **aiocoap** make it easy to integrate Python with IoT systems.

Key Libraries/Technologies:

- **RPi.GPIO** for controlling Raspberry Pi GPIO pins.
- **MicroPython** for embedded systems.
- **Paho MQTT** for messaging in IoT applications.
- **Flask** or **FastAPI** for building simple APIs for IoT devices.

4. How Python Supports Modern Development Paradigms like Microservices and Serverless Architectures

In addition to its presence in AI and IoT, Python is increasingly used in **modern development paradigms** like **microservices** and **serverless architectures**, which are becoming essential for scalable and efficient cloud-based systems.

- **Microservices**: Microservices is an architectural style where applications are composed of small, loosely-coupled services, each responsible for a single business function. Python works well with microservices due to its lightweight frameworks (such as **Flask** and **FastAPI**) and its strong support for **RESTful APIs**. Containers (using **Docker**) and orchestration tools (like **Kubernetes**) are often used to deploy Python-based microservices.

  Example: A Python microservice might handle user authentication while another service handles payment processing. Each service can be written in Python, with different services interacting through REST APIs.

- **Serverless Architectures**: In a **serverless architecture**, developers write code that runs in response to events, without worrying about the underlying infrastructure. Python is a popular language for **serverless computing**, especially on platforms like **AWS Lambda**, **Azure Functions**, and **Google Cloud Functions**.

  Example: A Python function can be triggered by an HTTP request or a file being uploaded to an S3 bucket. The serverless framework takes care of scaling, managing, and running the function in the cloud.

Key Libraries/Technologies:

- **Flask** and **FastAPI** for building RESTful APIs for microservices.
- **Docker** for containerizing Python-based microservices.
- **AWS Lambda**, **Google Cloud Functions**, and **Azure Functions** for serverless deployments.
- **Celery** for asynchronous task management.

5. Real-World Example: Developing a Python-Based Microservice for a Large-Scale Web Application

Let's walk through an example of developing a **microservice** in Python that could be used in a large-scale web application. Suppose we are building a **user authentication service** as a microservice for a web application.

Step 1: Set Up a Python Web Framework

We'll use **FastAPI** for this example, as it's lightweight and ideal for building fast, asynchronous APIs.

bash

```
pip install fastapi uvicorn
```

Step 2: Write the Authentication Microservice

python

```
from fastapi import FastAPI, HTTPException
from pydantic import BaseModel

app = FastAPI()

# A simple in-memory database of users
```

```python
users_db = {}

class User(BaseModel):
    username: str
    password: str


@app.post("/register/")
async def register(user: User):
    if user.username in users_db:
        raise HTTPException(status_code=400,
detail="Username already taken")
    users_db[user.username] = user.password
    return {"msg": "User registered
successfully"}


@app.post("/login/")
async def login(user: User):
    if user.username not in users_db or
users_db[user.username] != user.password:
        raise HTTPException(status_code=401,
detail="Invalid credentials")
    return {"msg": "Login successful"}
```

Step 3: Run the Microservice

We can run the microservice using **Uvicorn**, an ASGI server:

```bash
bash
```

```
uvicorn app:app --reload
```

This starts the authentication microservice, which exposes endpoints for registering and logging in users.

Step 4: Deploy the Microservice with Docker

To deploy this microservice, we can containerize it using **Docker**:

1. Create a `Dockerfile`:

```
dockerfile

FROM python:3.9-slim

WORKDIR /app

. /app

RUN pip install --no-cache-dir -r requirements.txt

CMD ["uvicorn", "app:app", "--host", "0.0.0.0", "--port", "8000"]
```

2. Build the Docker image:

```bash
bash
```

```
docker build -t auth-microservice .
```

3. Run the container:

```bash
bash
```

```
docker   run   -d   -p   8000:8000   auth-
microservice
```

Step 5: Integration into a Larger Web Application

This microservice can now be integrated into a larger web application. For example, the main application might communicate with this microservice via HTTP requests to handle user authentication.

In this chapter, we explored Python's evolving role in **modern software development** across several key domains, including **web development, artificial intelligence, IoT,** and cutting-edge paradigms like **microservices** and **serverless architectures**. Python's **simplicity, cross-platform capabilities,** and **rich ecosystem of libraries**

285

make it an ideal choice for developers working in these fields.

We also went through a **real-world example** of building a **microservice** for user authentication using **FastAPI**, showing how Python can be used to create scalable, modular components in modern web applications.

By understanding Python's role in these domains and leveraging the right frameworks and tools, developers can build flexible, efficient, and cross-platform applications that meet the demands of today's rapidly evolving technology landscape.

Chapter 24

Cloud Development and Python

Using Python for Cloud Development with AWS, Azure, and Google Cloud

Cloud computing has become an essential part of modern software development, offering scalable infrastructure, cost-efficiency, and flexibility. Python, with its rich ecosystem of libraries and tools, has become a go-to language for building **cloud applications** across different platforms, including **Amazon Web Services (AWS)**, **Microsoft Azure**, and **Google Cloud Platform (GCP)**.

In this chapter, we will explore how Python is used in cloud development with the three major cloud platforms: **AWS**, **Azure**, and **Google Cloud**. We will cover the basics of working with each platform and demonstrate how Python can be leveraged to build and deploy cross-platform cloud applications. Finally, we will walk through a **real-world example** of creating a **serverless application on AWS** using Python.

1. Using Python for Cloud Development with AWS

Amazon Web Services (AWS) is one of the most widely used cloud platforms for hosting and managing applications. Python can be used with AWS through the **Boto3** SDK, which allows developers to interact with various AWS services such as **EC2**, **S3**, **Lambda**, **DynamoDB**, and more.

- **Key Features**:
    - **Boto3**: The official AWS SDK for Python, which makes it easy to interact with AWS services.
    - **AWS Lambda**: A serverless compute service where you can run Python functions in response to events like HTTP requests, database changes, or file uploads to S3.
    - **Amazon EC2**: Allows you to provision virtual servers on demand for running Python applications.
    - **Amazon S3**: Object storage service where Python can be used to upload, download, and manage files.

Example: Deploying a Python-based Lambda function

1. **Install Boto3**:

```bash
pip install boto3
```

2. **Creating a Lambda Function**: Python can be used to create AWS Lambda functions, which can be triggered by events like API requests or file uploads.

```python
import json

def lambda_handler(event, context):
    message = "Hello from Lambda!"
    return {
        'statusCode': 200,
        'body': json.dumps(message)
    }
```

3. **Deploying the Lambda Function**: Lambda functions can be deployed directly via the AWS Management Console or through **AWS CLI** and **Boto3**.

2. Using Python for Cloud Development with Azure

Microsoft Azure is another leading cloud platform, offering a wide range of services like virtual machines, databases, AI tools, and more. Python is supported through the **Azure SDK for Python**, which allows developers to interact with various Azure services.

- **Key Features**:
  - o **Azure Functions**: Azure's serverless compute offering, similar to AWS Lambda, that allows you to run Python code in response to events.
  - o **Azure Blob Storage**: Object storage service where Python can be used to upload and manage files.
  - o **Azure App Services**: A platform-as-a-service (PaaS) for hosting web applications, including Python-based apps.
  - o **Azure Databases**: Python can be used with Azure databases like **SQL Database** or **Cosmos DB** for data storage and management.

Example: Deploying a Python Function with Azure Functions

1. **Install Azure Functions SDK**:

```bash
bash

pip install azure-functions
```

2. **Creating an Azure Function**:

```python
python

import azure.functions as func

def main(req: func.HttpRequest) ->
func.HttpResponse:
    name = req.params.get('name')
    if not name:
        return func.HttpResponse(
            "Please pass a name on the
query string",
            status_code=400
        )
    return func.HttpResponse(f"Hello
{name}!", status_code=200)
```

3. **Deploying to Azure**: You can deploy Python functions directly to Azure using the **Azure Functions Core Tools** or the **Azure CLI**.

291

3. Using Python for Cloud Development with Google Cloud

Google Cloud Platform (GCP) provides powerful infrastructure and services for building, deploying, and scaling applications. Python is widely used in **Google Cloud Functions**, **App Engine**, **Cloud Storage**, and **BigQuery**, among other services.

- **Key Features**:
    - o **Google Cloud Functions**: Serverless computing platform similar to AWS Lambda and Azure Functions, enabling you to run Python code in response to events.
    - o **Google Cloud Storage**: Object storage that can be managed with Python for file uploads and downloads.
    - o **Google App Engine**: Platform-as-a-service for deploying web applications, including Python-based apps.
    - o **BigQuery**: A fully managed data warehouse for analyzing large datasets using SQL and Python libraries.

Example: Deploying a Python Function on Google Cloud Functions

1. **Install Google Cloud SDK**:

   bash

   ```
   pip install google-cloud-functions
   ```

2. **Creating a Cloud Function**:

   python

   ```
   def hello_world(request):
       return 'Hello, World!'
   ```

3. **Deploying to Google Cloud**: Use the **Google Cloud Console** or **gcloud CLI** to deploy your Python function to Google Cloud Functions.

---

4. Building and Deploying Cross-Platform Cloud Applications with Python

Building **cross-platform cloud applications** with Python typically involves using cloud providers' SDKs or services (such as **AWS Lambda**, **Azure Functions**, and **Google Cloud Functions**) and integrating them with other cloud services (e.g., databases, storage, messaging systems). Python provides a consistent development experience,

293

allowing you to deploy your application across different cloud platforms without making significant changes to the codebase.

Common Steps for Building Cross-Platform Cloud Applications:

1. **Choose a Cloud Provider**: Decide whether to use **AWS**, **Azure**, or **Google Cloud** for your cloud infrastructure.

2. **Use Python SDKs**: Leverage the Python SDKs (e.g., **Boto3** for AWS, **azure-functions** for Azure, and **google-cloud** for GCP) to interact with cloud services.

3. **Write Cloud-Ready Code**: Ensure your Python application is modular, stateless, and can run in a serverless environment.

4. **Use Docker**: For more complex applications, containerizing your Python application using Docker ensures portability across cloud platforms.

5. **Deploy**: Deploy your application to your cloud provider using services like **Lambda** (AWS), **Azure Functions**, or **Google Cloud Functions**.

Let's walk through creating a simple **serverless application** on **AWS** using **Python**. We will build a Python-based Lambda function that is triggered by an API Gateway request.

Step 1: Setting Up AWS Lambda Function

1. **Create the Lambda function**: Go to the **AWS Management Console**, select **Lambda**, and create a new function. Choose **Author from Scratch** and set the runtime to **Python 3.8**.

2. **Write the Lambda function**: Use the following code for the Lambda function that returns a greeting message.

```python
python

import json

def lambda_handler(event, context):
    name                              =
event.get('queryStringParameters',
{}).get('name', 'World')
    return {
```

295

```
        'statusCode': 200,
        'body':         json.dumps(f'Hello,
{name}!')
            }
```

Explanation:

- This Lambda function reads the `name` parameter from the query string and returns a greeting message. If no name is provided, it defaults to `"World"`.

Step 2: Set Up API Gateway

1. **Create an API Gateway**: Go to **API Gateway** in the AWS Console and create a new **REST API**.

2. **Integrate API Gateway with Lambda**: Set up a method (e.g., **GET**) for the API and link it to the Lambda function you created. Deploy the API and note the endpoint URL.

Step 3: Test the Lambda Function

Once the function is deployed, you can test it by calling the API using the endpoint URL:

bash

```
https://<api-id>.execute-
api.<region>.amazonaws.com/Prod/hello?name=Pyth
on
```

This will trigger the Lambda function and return the message:

```json
"Hello, Python!"
```

In this chapter, we explored Python's role in **cloud development** across different platforms like **AWS**, **Azure**, and **Google Cloud**. We discussed how Python can be used with cloud services like **Lambda** (AWS), **Functions** (Azure), and **Cloud Functions** (GCP), as well as how to build and deploy **cross-platform cloud applications** using Python.

We also went through a **real-world example** of creating a **serverless application on AWS** using Python. This example demonstrated how to build a Lambda function that is triggered by an API Gateway request, providing a simple yet powerful way to deploy serverless applications in the cloud.

By leveraging Python's flexibility and powerful cloud SDKs, you can create scalable, efficient, and cross-platform cloud applications that run seamlessly across major cloud platforms. Whether you're building serverless applications, microservices, or integrating with cloud storage and databases, Python provides the tools needed to take full advantage of the cloud.

Chapter 25

Python in IoT Development

How Python is Used for Developing IoT Applications That Can Run Across Platforms

The **Internet of Things (IoT)** refers to the network of physical devices that are connected to the internet and can collect, exchange, and act on data. Python, with its simplicity and versatility, is an excellent choice for developing **IoT applications**. Its cross-platform nature and extensive libraries make it ideal for building solutions that work across various hardware devices and operating systems, from embedded systems (like microcontrollers) to cloud platforms.

In this chapter, we will explore how Python is used for developing **cross-platform IoT applications**, how Python libraries enable interaction with sensors and devices, and how Python can communicate with **networks**. We will also walk through a **real-world example** of building an IoT project using Python to monitor **environmental data** from multiple devices.

1. Python in IoT Development

Python has become increasingly popular in the **IoT** space for several reasons:

- **Ease of Use**: Python's readable syntax makes it ideal for rapid development, allowing developers to prototype and deploy IoT solutions quickly.
- **Cross-Platform**: Python runs on a wide variety of platforms, including **Raspberry Pi**, **Arduino**, **BeagleBone**, **Linux**, and **Windows**, making it suitable for a wide range of IoT applications.
- **Large Ecosystem of Libraries**: Python offers a rich set of libraries and frameworks that facilitate communication with sensors, devices, and networks. These libraries enable Python to interact with a wide variety of hardware, including sensors, actuators, and wireless networks.

Python's role in IoT spans across various areas, including:

- **Data Collection**: Gathering data from sensors or devices.
- **Data Processing**: Processing and analyzing the data locally or remotely.

- **Communication**: Sending data over the network or to the cloud.
- **Automation**: Taking actions based on sensor readings or external inputs.

2. Python Libraries for Working with Sensors, Devices, and Networks

Python provides a variety of libraries for interfacing with **IoT sensors**, controlling **devices**, and enabling communication over **networks**. Some of the most widely used libraries include:

1. `RPi.GPIO` (for Raspberry Pi GPIO pins):

- **RPi.GPIO** is the standard library used to interact with the General Purpose Input/Output (GPIO) pins on the **Raspberry Pi**, which are commonly used for interfacing with sensors and devices.
- **Common Use Cases**:
    - Reading inputs from sensors (e.g., temperature, motion).
    - Controlling output devices (e.g., LEDs, motors).

Example:

```python
python

import RPi.GPIO as GPIO
import time

GPIO.setmode(GPIO.BCM)
GPIO.setup(18, GPIO.OUT)

# Blink an LED
while True:
    GPIO.output(18, GPIO.HIGH)
    time.sleep(1)
    GPIO.output(18, GPIO.LOW)
    time.sleep(1)
```

2. `Adafruit_CircuitPython` Libraries:

- **Adafruit** provides a series of Python libraries for working with various sensors, displays, and other devices. These libraries are particularly useful for **Raspberry Pi** and **Arduino** development.
- **Common Use Cases:**
    - Reading from sensors like temperature sensors (e.g., **DHT22**), light sensors, and accelerometers.
    - Controlling devices like **displays** and **motors**.

Example:

```python

import board
import adafruit_dht

# Set up the sensor
dhtDevice = adafruit_dht.DHT22(board.D4)

while True:
    try:
        temperature = dhtDevice.temperature
        humidity = dhtDevice.humidity
        print(f"Temperature:    {temperature}C,
Humidity: {humidity}%")
    except RuntimeError as error:
        print(error.args[0])
    time.sleep(2)
```

3. pySerial (for serial communication):

- **pySerial** is a library used to communicate with devices over **serial ports** (UART, USB, etc.). It's often used for **Arduino** communication or to interface with other microcontrollers and devices.

- **Common Use Cases**:

    o Communicating with **Arduino** or other microcontrollers via USB or Bluetooth.

o Sending and receiving data between Python and embedded systems.

Example:

```python
python

import serial

# Set up the serial connection
ser = serial.Serial('/dev/ttyUSB0', 9600)

# Send data
ser.write(b'Hello, IoT!\n')

# Read data
data = ser.readline()
print(data)
```

4. paho-mqtt (for MQTT protocol):

- **MQTT** (Message Queuing Telemetry Transport) is a lightweight, publish/subscribe messaging protocol commonly used in IoT for communication between devices and servers.
- **paho-mqtt** is a Python library for implementing MQTT clients and brokers.
- **Common Use Cases:**

- o Sending sensor data from devices to a server or cloud service.
- o Receiving commands or updates to control IoT devices.

Example (sending data to a broker):

```python

import paho.mqtt.client as mqtt

# Define the callback function
def on_connect(client, userdata, flags, rc):
    print("Connected   with   result   code   "   +
str(rc))
    client.publish("home/temperature",
payload="22.5", qos=0, retain=False)

# Set up MQTT client
client = mqtt.Client()
client.on_connect = on_connect
client.connect("mqtt.eclipse.org", 1883, 60)

# Loop forever
client.loop_forever()
```

5. requests (for HTTP communication):

- The **requests** library is widely used for making HTTP requests, which is useful for **cloud communication**, web APIs, or communicating with RESTful services.
- **Common Use Cases**:
    - Sending data to a cloud service via HTTP POST requests.
    - Receiving configuration or command data from a server.

Example:

```python
import requests

# Sending data to a web API
response                                    =
requests.post("http://example.com/data",
json={"temperature": 22.5, "humidity": 60})
print(response.status_code)
```

3. Real-World Example: Building an IoT Project Using Python to Monitor Environmental Data from Multiple Devices

Let's build a simple **IoT project** using Python where we will monitor **environmental data** (temperature and humidity) from **multiple devices** (Raspberry Pis with DHT22 sensors) and send this data to a central server via **MQTT**.

Step 1: Set Up the Environment

1. Install the necessary libraries:

```bash
pip install paho-mqtt adafruit-circuitpython-dht RPi.GPIO
```

2. Set up the Raspberry Pi devices with **DHT22 sensors** connected to **GPIO pins**.

Step 2: Write Code to Collect Data from Sensors

```python
import time
import paho.mqtt.client as mqtt
import adafruit_dht
import RPi.GPIO as GPIO
import board

# Initialize the sensor
dhtDevice = adafruit_dht.DHT22(board.D4)

# MQTT client setup
```

```python
client = mqtt.Client()
client.connect("mqtt.eclipse.org", 1883, 60)

# Function to read sensor and publish to MQTT
def read_and_publish():
    try:
        temperature = dhtDevice.temperature
        humidity = dhtDevice.humidity
        print(f"Temperature:      {temperature}C,
Humidity: {humidity}%")

        # Publish data to MQTT
        client.publish("home/temperature",
payload=temperature)
        client.publish("home/humidity",
payload=humidity)
    except RuntimeError as error:
        print(error.args[0])

# Main loop
while True:
    read_and_publish()
    time.sleep(10)   # Wait for 10 seconds before
reading again
```

Explanation:

- This code reads the **temperature** and **humidity** data from a **DHT22 sensor** connected to a Raspberry Pi.

- It then sends the data to an **MQTT broker** (mqtt.eclipse.org in this case).
- The data is published to two separate topics: **home/temperature** and **home/humidity**.

Step 3: Monitor the Data from Multiple Devices

You can deploy the same Python script on **multiple Raspberry Pi devices** (or any IoT devices) that will each monitor their local environment (temperature and humidity) and send the data to the **central MQTT broker**.

Step 4: Set Up a Centralized System to Receive and Process the Data

A simple **MQTT subscriber** in Python can be used to monitor the topics and print out the data from multiple devices:

```python
import paho.mqtt.client as mqtt

# Define the callback function for receiving
messages
def on_message(client, userdata, msg):
```

```
    print(f"Topic:      {msg.topic},      Message:
{msg.payload.decode()}")

# Set up MQTT client
client = mqtt.Client()
client.on_message = on_message
client.connect("mqtt.eclipse.org", 1883, 60)

# Subscribe to the temperature and humidity
topics
client.subscribe("home/temperature")
client.subscribe("home/humidity")

# Start the MQTT loop to receive messages
client.loop_forever()
```

Explanation:

- This script subscribes to the **home/temperature** and
  home/humidity topics on the MQTT broker.
- It prints out the data received from each device
  whenever a new message is published.

In this chapter, we explored how Python can be used to
develop **cross-platform IoT applications** that interact with

sensors, **devices**, and **networks**. We covered the use of Python libraries like **RPi.GPIO**, **Adafruit CircuitPython**, **pySerial**, and **paho-mqtt**, which allow Python to interface with IoT hardware and communicate with the cloud or other devices.

Through the **real-world example**, we built a Python-based IoT project that monitors environmental data from multiple devices and sends the data to a central server via MQTT. This project illustrates how Python can be used to collect data from sensors, process it, and communicate with other devices or systems in an efficient and cross-platform manner.

By utilizing Python's flexibility and wide range of libraries, developers can easily create powerful and scalable IoT solutions, whether it's for **home automation**, **environmental monitoring**, or more complex IoT systems.

Chapter 26

Ethical and Sustainable Python Development

Addressing Ethical Concerns in Python Development and the Importance of Sustainable Software Engineering Practices

As Python continues to grow in popularity, it's crucial for developers to consider the **ethical implications** of the software they create and the **sustainability** of the development practices they employ. Ethical software development not only concerns the societal and environmental impacts of the software but also involves ensuring fairness, inclusivity, and responsible use of technology. Similarly, sustainable practices in software engineering focus on minimizing the resource consumption, including energy, memory, and time, of software applications.

This chapter will delve into the ethical issues that can arise in Python development, the importance of adopting sustainable software engineering practices, and how Python can play a crucial role in **green computing**. Finally, we will look at a **real-world example** where Python is used to develop an application that supports **sustainable practices**.

1. Ethical Concerns in Python Development

Ethics in software development goes beyond just coding practices. It encompasses how software is designed, used, and the impacts it has on users and society. Ethical concerns in Python development are no different and include issues such as:

- **Data Privacy and Security**: Protecting users' data is one of the primary ethical responsibilities of developers. Python developers should ensure that their applications are secure, with proper encryption, secure data handling, and transparent privacy policies.
    - o **Example**: When handling personal or sensitive data (e.g., healthcare information or financial data), Python developers should follow best practices for **data encryption** and ensure that the **user consent** is obtained before processing the data.

- **Bias in Algorithms**: Machine learning and AI, areas where Python is heavily used, are susceptible to biases. If the data used to train algorithms is biased, the algorithm's decisions will be biased too, leading to unfair or discriminatory outcomes.

  o **Example**: When developing AI applications, it's essential to ensure that the data used is representative and that model decisions are transparent and explainable. Python developers should strive for fairness by identifying and mitigating bias in data and algorithms.

- **Access and Inclusivity**: Ethical software must also be **inclusive**. Python developers should ensure that their software is accessible to people with disabilities and users from diverse backgrounds.

  o **Example**: Designing web applications with accessibility features (e.g., text-to-speech, high contrast themes, or screen reader support) is important for inclusivity.

- **Software for Social Good**: Developers can also contribute to social good by creating software that addresses societal challenges, such as **public health**, **environmental sustainability**, or **education**.

Green computing refers to the practice of designing, developing, and using computing resources in an environmentally responsible way. With the rise of IoT, cloud computing, and data-driven applications, the environmental impact of software is becoming more significant. Python, due to its versatility and widespread usage, plays a key role in promoting green computing practices.

Energy-Efficient Algorithms: Energy efficiency is a critical aspect of sustainability in Python development. The goal is to reduce the energy consumption of software while maintaining performance. This includes optimizing algorithms, reducing resource usage, and utilizing hardware resources effectively.

- **Optimizing Algorithms**: By choosing more efficient algorithms (in terms of time and space complexity), developers can reduce the computational power required, which in turn minimizes energy consumption.
  - **Example**: A Python developer can reduce the number of database queries in a web application

315

by optimizing SQL queries or caching results, leading to lower server load and reduced energy usage.

- **Green Cloud Computing**: Many organizations are moving to the cloud, which leads to massive energy consumption by data centers. Python developers can help reduce this impact by writing efficient code that minimizes server usage, choosing **green cloud providers** (those who use renewable energy), and leveraging cloud-based **auto-scaling** to match resource consumption to actual demand.

  o **Example**: Instead of running heavy computations continuously, a Python-based application can be set up to run only when necessary, scaling cloud resources dynamically.

- **Low-Power Devices**: In IoT, energy-efficient Python code running on low-power devices like **Raspberry Pi** or **Arduino** is important for reducing the overall energy footprint of connected devices.

  o **Example**: Python code for IoT applications running on microcontrollers can be optimized to ensure minimal energy consumption while maintaining functionality.

3. Real-World Example: Developing a Python Application that Supports Sustainable Practices, Such as Energy Consumption Monitoring

Let's create a simple **energy consumption monitoring** application in Python that can help users track and reduce their energy usage, contributing to sustainability efforts.

In this project, we will use **Python** to read **energy meter data** (either from sensors or a public API), process the data, and display it in a user-friendly format. This will allow users to track their energy consumption and take steps to reduce it, thereby supporting sustainable energy practices.

Step 1: Set Up the Energy Meter Data Source

For this example, let's assume we have an energy meter that provides data in a simple JSON format via a public API.

json

```
{
    "timestamp": "2025-02-16T12:00:00",
    "current_usage": 450,  # in watts
    "daily_consumption": 10,  # in kWh
    "monthly_consumption": 300  # in kWh
}
```

317

Step 2: Write Python Code to Fetch and Process the Data

We will write a Python script that fetches energy data from an API, processes it, and displays the information.

```python
import requests
import json

# Fetch energy data from a public API
def get_energy_data(api_url):
    response = requests.get(api_url)
    if response.status_code == 200:
        return response.json()
    else:
        print("Error fetching data")
        return None

# Process energy data
def process_energy_data(data):
    current_usage = data['current_usage']
    daily_consumption             =
data['daily_consumption']
    monthly_consumption           =
data['monthly_consumption']

    print(f"Current Usage: {current_usage}W")
```

```
    print(f"Daily                Consumption:
{daily_consumption} kWh")
    print(f"Monthly               Consumption:
{monthly_consumption} kWh")


# Example API URL
api_url                                    =
"https://api.example.com/energy_meter_data"
energy_data = get_energy_data(api_url)
if energy_data:
    process_energy_data(energy_data)
```

Explanation:

- The `get_energy_data` function fetches the data from the energy meter API.
- The `process_energy_data` function processes the fetched data and prints it in a user-friendly format.

Step 3: Displaying the Data in a User-Friendly Format

To make the application more interactive and usable, we can add a simple **graphical user interface (GUI)** using **Tkinter** or **Flask** (for web applications). Below is a basic example using **Tkinter** to display the energy data:

```
python
```

```python
import tkinter as tk

# Create a simple Tkinter window to display
energy data
def create_window(data):
    root = tk.Tk()
    root.title("Energy Consumption Monitor")

    label1 = tk.Label(root, text=f"Current
Usage: {data['current_usage']}W")
    label1.pack()

    label2 = tk.Label(root, text=f"Daily
Consumption: {data['daily_consumption']} kWh")
    label2.pack()

    label3 = tk.Label(root, text=f"Monthly
Consumption: {data['monthly_consumption']} kWh")
    label3.pack()

    root.mainloop()

# Display the energy data
if energy_data:
    create_window(energy_data)
```

Step 4: Optimizing for Sustainability

320

1. **Efficient Code**: The application fetches energy data only when necessary (for example, every hour), preventing unnecessary API calls that could lead to excessive energy consumption by the server.

2. **Optimizing Performance**: We ensure the application processes data efficiently without unnecessary loops or memory usage.

3. **User Engagement**: The application encourages users to monitor their energy usage regularly and make informed decisions about their consumption, contributing to sustainability.

In this chapter, we explored the **ethical and sustainable practices** in Python development. We discussed the importance of addressing ethical concerns such as **data privacy**, **algorithmic fairness**, and **inclusive software**. Additionally, we examined how Python can contribute to **green computing** and **energy-efficient algorithms** in areas like **cloud computing** and **IoT development**.

We also developed a **real-world example** of a Python application that monitors **energy consumption**. This application not only demonstrates how Python can be used to support **sustainable practices**, but also highlights the importance of optimizing software to reduce environmental impact.

By embracing ethical and sustainable development practices, Python developers can contribute to a greener and more equitable future, creating software that is not only powerful and efficient but also responsible and environmentally conscious.

Chapter 27

Becoming a Global Python Developer

How to Continue Learning and Growing as a Python Developer

Becoming a proficient **Python developer** is a continuous journey that requires dedication, curiosity, and a passion for learning. While Python is renowned for its simplicity and accessibility, mastering it and becoming an expert, particularly in cross-platform development, takes practice and hands-on experience. To stay competitive and continue growing as a Python developer, here are a few strategies you can adopt:

1. **Work on Real Projects**:
   - The best way to solidify your Python skills is by working on real-world projects. Build projects that align with your interests, such as web applications, data analysis, IoT systems, or even cross-platform mobile apps. Working on tangible projects will expose you to common development challenges, and you'll learn how to solve them efficiently.

2. **Stay Updated with New Features**:

o Python evolves constantly, with new versions introducing new features and optimizations. Make it a habit to stay up to date with the latest releases and enhancements. Regularly reading **Python Enhancement Proposals (PEPs)**, following Python-related blogs, and attending webinars or conferences are good ways to keep yourself informed.

3. **Learn Python Internals**:

o For advanced developers, learning how Python works under the hood can significantly improve your programming practices. Dive deeper into how Python handles memory management, the **Global Interpreter Lock (GIL)**, and the **Python Virtual Machine (PVM)**. Understanding these concepts will help you write more efficient and optimized code.

4. **Expand Your Knowledge in Specialized Areas**:

o Python is used in many specialized domains such as **machine learning**, **data science**, **networking**, **automation**, and **web development**. If you want to become an expert, consider diving deeper into one of these fields. Learn more about libraries and frameworks specific to those areas like **TensorFlow**, **Flask**, **Django**, or **Pandas**.

5. **Practice Code Refactoring**:

   o Python is known for clean and readable code. However, even the most elegant solutions can be improved. Constantly refactor your code to make it more efficient, modular, and readable. This will sharpen your skills and make you a better developer in the long run.

Resources for Furthering Your Knowledge of Cross-Platform Development and Python

There are numerous resources available to help you further your knowledge and expertise in Python, particularly in the area of **cross-platform development**. These resources will allow you to deepen your understanding, explore new tools, and stay updated with industry trends.

1. **Official Python Documentation**:

   o The Python documentation is the most authoritative and comprehensive source for learning about the language. It covers everything from basic syntax to advanced topics, and it's constantly updated with the latest features and best practices.

2. **Books**:

- ○ **"Fluent Python" by Luciano Ramalho**: A deep dive into Python for experienced developers.

- ○ **"Python for Data Analysis" by Wes McKinney**: A great resource for Python developers working with data science.

- ○ **"Python Crash Course" by Eric Matthes**: A beginner-friendly book that covers fundamental concepts and practical applications.

- ○ **"Automate the Boring Stuff with Python" by Al Sweigart**: Perfect for Python beginners looking to make the most of Python for everyday tasks.

3. **Online Platforms**:

- ○ **Real Python**: Offers tutorials, articles, and courses for Python developers of all levels.

- ○ **PyBites**: Provides coding challenges and exercises to improve Python skills.

- ○ **Udemy and Coursera**: Have many Python courses ranging from beginner to expert level, with a focus on various aspects like web development, machine learning, and IoT.

4. **Cross-Platform Development Resources**:

- ○ **Kivy** (for mobile and desktop apps): Kivy Documentation for learning how to build cross-platform UIs.

- o **PyQt**: The PyQt Documentation provides detailed guides on how to create desktop applications for multiple platforms.

- o **Docker**: Learning **Docker** is crucial for developing and deploying cross-platform applications. The Docker Documentation is an excellent place to start.

- o **Tox**: A tool for testing across multiple environments. The Tox Documentation will help you set up automated testing for cross-platform apps.

5. **Podcasts and YouTube Channels**:

- o **Talk Python to Me**: A podcast that covers Python news, best practices, and interviews with Python experts.

- o **Python Weekly**: A weekly newsletter that curates Python news, tutorials, and articles.

- o **Python Programming (YouTube)**: Channels like **Corey Schafer** and **Tech With Tim** are excellent for learning practical Python programming and projects.

Building a Career as a Global Python Developer and Contributing to Open-Source Projects

As Python continues to be one of the most in-demand programming languages in the world, building a successful career as a **global Python developer** is more achievable than ever. Here are some ways you can build a career and contribute to the Python ecosystem:

1. **Contribute to Open Source Projects**:
    - o Open-source contributions are a great way to improve your Python skills while giving back to the community. Python has a vast open-source ecosystem, and you can contribute by improving documentation, fixing bugs, or developing new features for existing libraries.
    - o Websites like **GitHub** and **GitLab** host thousands of open-source Python projects that you can contribute to. You can also explore Python-specific repositories like **python/cpython** (Python's official repo) or libraries like **Django**, **Flask**, and **Pandas**.

2. **Build a Strong Portfolio**:
    - o Having a well-rounded portfolio is essential to showcasing your Python skills. Include diverse

projects that demonstrate your ability to work with various Python libraries and frameworks. This can include projects related to **web development**, **data science**, **IoT**, and **cross-platform applications**.

- o Use **GitHub** to host your code and make it publicly available to potential employers or collaborators.

3. **Networking and Collaboration**:

- o Attend Python conferences like **PyCon**, **EuroPython**, and **local meetups** to network with other Python developers, share knowledge, and find opportunities.

- o Participate in online communities like **Stack Overflow**, **Reddit's Python Subreddit**, and Python Discord servers to ask questions, collaborate, and learn from others.

4. **Freelancing and Remote Work**:

- o Python developers are highly sought after for remote work and freelance opportunities. Websites like **Upwork**, **Freelancer**, and **Toptal** offer platforms for Python developers to find freelance projects.

- o You can also work as a full-time remote Python developer for companies across the globe. This allows you to work on international projects while enjoying the flexibility of working from anywhere.

5. **Teaching and Mentoring**:

   o Teaching others is one of the best ways to reinforce your understanding of Python. Consider writing blog posts, creating tutorial videos, or even teaching Python online. Websites like **Udemy**, **Coursera**, and **YouTube** offer platforms where you can share your expertise with a global audience.

   o Mentoring junior developers can help you develop leadership skills while contributing to the Python community.

In this chapter, we discussed how to continue growing as a **Python developer** by engaging with various learning resources, contributing to open-source projects, and building a career as a **global Python developer**. As the Python ecosystem continues to evolve and expand, the opportunities for developers will continue to grow, both in terms of technology and career prospects.

By continuing to learn, contribute to open-source projects, and build a strong portfolio, you can ensure that you stay relevant and successful in the ever-changing world of Python development. Whether you are working on cutting-edge technologies or building simple scripts, Python's versatility allows you to make an impact on projects that improve businesses, communities, and the world at large.

www.ingramcontent.com/pod-product-compliance
Lightning Source LLC
LaVergne TN
LVHW022334060326
832902LV00022B/4031